WESTERN SCIENCE IN THE ARAB WORLD

WESTERN SCIENCE IN THE ARAB WORLD

The Impact of Darwinism, 1860–1930

Adel A. Ziadat

Assistant Professor of Journalism and Mass Communication,
Yarmouk University, Irbid, Jordan

St. Martin's Press   New York

First published in the United States of America in 1986

Printed in Hong Kong

ISBN 0-312-86433-7

Library of Congress Cataloging-in-Publication Data
Ziadat, Adel A., 1944–
Western science in the Arab world.
Bibliography: p.
Includes index.
1. Science—Arab countries.   2. Science—Moral and
ethical aspects.   3. Darwin, Charles, 1809–1882.
I. Title.
Q127.A5Z53   1986   509.17'4   85-27929
ISBN 0-312-86433-7

*To my parents
for their love and interest in education*

Contents

Acknowledgements

I gratefully acknowledge my obligation to the many who were helpful at one stage or another during the writing of this dissertation.

I wish to express my gratitude to Professor Lewis Pyenson, who supervised this work. Professor Pyenson has been resourceful, patient and encouraging. I was fortunate to have had the opportunity to work under his guidance.

Professors Ibrahim Yousef of l'Université de Montréal and Ayman al-Yassini of Concordia University provided many helpful comments on an earlier version of this study. I am appreciative of their assistance.

In the United States, Britain and the Middle East scholars provided valuable suggestions for the location of research material and encouraging remarks on an earlier draft proposal of this thesis. I am indebted to Professors Hisham Sharabi of Georgetown University, Antoin Zahlan in Britain and Ali Kettani, Director General of the Islamic Foundation for Science and Technology for Development in Saudi Arabia.

I profited from talking with Professors Othmar Keel and Yakov Rabkin, who brought to my attention various bibliographical items of interest to this work.

My thanks go to my brothers, Nwir and Ahed, to my sister Diya and to Carmen, Rita, Michelina and Rosa Della-Civita for moral support and for their unsparing efforts in searching for some material not available in North American Libraries.

The staffs of the H. Gibb and Widener Libraries of Harvard University were most generous in making available their resources.

A. A. Z.

Note on Transliteration and Translation

Arabic names and words are given in the form usually accepted in English. In general, the system adopted in the *Journal for the History of Arabic Science* is followed with slight variations. For example, *hamzah* and *ain* at the beginning of a word are omitted. The lam of the Arabic article before sun-letters is not assimilated; therefore, I write 'al-shams' and not 'ash-shams'.

During my period of study, many journals and books appeared entirely in Arabic. While many non-Arabic speaking writers contributed to these journals, their writings were always translated into Arabic. I have responded to this special problem by using the commonly accepted spelling for Arab places instead of a transliteration. Thus, the reader will see 'Beirut' and 'Lebanon' instead of 'Bayrut' and 'Lubnan', and 'Louis Cheikho' and 'Hussein' instead of 'Luwis Shaykhu' and 'Husayn'. In reporting texts and titles, transliteration follows the rules adopted by the *Journal for the History of Arabic Science*.

All dates are given according to the Christian calendar. Certain scientific or biological terms which appear in Arabic writings are transliterated between two brackets: 'tatawwur' (evolution).

Summary

The present study considers the introduction of Western science into the Arab world during the late nineteenth and early twentieth centuries, with special attention to the reception accorded to the writings of Charles Darwin. It shows that Arab scholars played central roles in identifying the scientific importance of Darwin's theories. It also shows that Arab thinkers had ideas and preoccupations similar to their Western counterparts. There was a polarization between religious and secularist thinkers, as might be expected. Yet a number of religious writers, both Christian and Muslim, sought to reach an accommodation with Darwin's theory of evolution. Muslim Shiites were, indeed, among the most reasonable interpreters of Darwin's thought. The major division among commentators was not between Christian and Muslim, but rather between agnostic and atheist writers on the one hand and religious writers on the other. Most Arab writers, religious or secularist, sought to use at least some of Darwin's discoveries to promote an awakened spirit of Arab nationalism.

During the first part of the nineteenth century, knowledge of modern science started infiltrating into the Arab world. Foreign ideas were not received uncritically, and a great debate began about the role of science in society and its relation to religion, especially Islam. Strong reaction was voiced by conservative elements, who were mainly concerned with preserving traditional values. As a result, controversies became common and provided an important stimulus for many Arab writings on different aspects of Western science, especially on Darwin's theory of evolution.

Chapter 1 describes the historical development of Arab educational institutions before and after the introduction of Western-style learning to the area. The purpose of this chapter is to provide a perspective for later discussion of the reception of Darwinism in the Arab world. It is shown that while the aim of missionary education was basically religious, some of the pioneering Arab minds – for example, teachers at the Syrian Protestant College – exhibited a strong commitment to introduce Western science into the Arab world. Much of the growth of early scientific knowledge took place in the early years of the Syrian College in conjunction with pioneering Arab efforts in introducing modern thought into the school system.

Chapter 2 examines the emergence of Darwinism in Arabic literature. It shows that while Darwin's ideas were first introduced in 1876 through the medium of *al-Muqtataf*, the full-fledged debate among Arab thinkers came after the translation and publication of Ludwig Büchner's commentary on Darwinism by Shibli Shumayyil in 1882. Together, the first two chapters lay the basis for Chapter 3 which analyses the major intellectual responses to the penetration of Darwin's ideas into the Arab world.

Chapter 3 discusses a number of Arabs who wrote in Arabic about science and Darwinism. The pattern that emerged from their writings illustrates a painful process of working through new Western ideas in order to arrive at a compromise with religion and traditional values. This chapter analyses the influence of Darwin's science on Arab Christian secular thought. It explains their ideas and ideologies regarding Darwinism, natural science and religion. The chapter discusses at length the manner in which these ideas were received by Arab Christians and how they reacted to Arab traditional tenets in the light of a new set of concepts. It shows that Arab thinkers adopted Darwinism *in toto* because of its progressive thought. They held that the progress of Arab society depended on complete adoption of Western science and values and believed that by the proper use of natural science, an Arab intellectual and moral renaissance could be brought about.

Chapter 4 discusses the responses of secularist Arabs to Darwinism and the controversies around it. The focus is on materialism and its impact on the morality of war. It also deals with Arab interpretations of the ideas of natural selection and survival of the fittest. It demonstrates the concern of Arab thinkers about the quality of foreign ideas, namely Darwin's ideas, which were introduced into their school system. It is shown that Arab writers were opposed to the use of Darwinian thought to justify wars and racial superiority over others. The challenge of Darwinism was not directed to practical affairs but to abstract ones.

Chapters 5 and 6 begin with a brief introduction to the climate of religious opinion that prevailed among Arab religious writers, both Muslims and Christians, at the end of the nineteenth century.

Chapter 5 examines religious Christian responses to Darwinism. The findings of science and Darwin's theory were viewed by some learned circles as contrary to the teaching of the Bible. They debated with Arab secularists the issues of animal intelligence, manna of the Jews, the star of Bethlehem and man's relationship to God and nature.

Chapter 6 examines the Muslim responses to Darwinism. It shows that Muslim Arab reaction to Darwinian thought was mixed. Some Muslim Arab thinkers provided a comprehensive account on the issues surrounding the Islamic religion regarding the new findings of biology. Like Christian Arabs, their main concern was how to reconcile their beliefs with modern evolutionary ideas on the creation of man and his position in the world.

1 Introduction

THE ARAB WORLD IN THE NINETEENTH CENTURY

The Arab world of today consists of twenty-two sovereign and non-sovereign Arab states which are members of the Arab League. With the exception of Morocco and Yemen, the Arab world entered the modern period as part of the Ottoman Empire. This Empire stretched from the Balkans to the Sudan and from Persia to the Atlas Mountains. In the major portion of the Arab provinces of the Empire, government affairs were conducted by a ruling elite of predominantly Turkish origin, while the language of communication among the Arab masses, as well as the language of instruction and culture, remained Arabic. The Turks tried at one time or another, during their rule over the Arab provinces, to displace Arabic with Turkish as a means of communication, but their attempt ultimately ended in failure. The Arab masses viewed themselves as segments of the Islamic *Ummah* (Community) headed by the Ottoman Caliph, but they committed themselves to the preservation of their Arab cultural identity.

In the Arab world, the nineteenth century has been called the century of Christian missions. This identification is due to the decline of Ottoman authority and the granting of concessions to foreign powers. Principal among these concessions was political protection provided to minority religious communities. This system practically invited large scale invasions by various missionary movements.

Nineteenth century Syria (which includes present-day Palestine, Israel, Lebanon, Jordan and present-day Syria) had long acted as a cultural and commercial link between the East and the West. Under the Islamic empire of the *Umaggads*, Syria was an active participant in the process of transmitting Greek science and philosophy to the Muslim world. Moreover, commercial contact with Europe was maintained even before the Crusades.[1]

Under Ottoman rule, Syrian and Lebanese merchants maintained

1

contact with the West long before the French occupation of Egypt in 1798 despite Ottoman attempts to impose physical and intellectual isolation on the Arab provinces. To provide only one example, the Lebanese Amir Fakhr al-Din al-Mani, 'allied himself with the Medici Court in Florence against his Suzerain, the Sublime Porte, sojourned in Italy for five years (1613–1618), and invited Italian technologists with know-how to develop the underdeveloped resources of his mountainous land'.[2]

It was nevertheless with Napoleon's invasion of Egypt and Palestine and its subsequent impact, that a massive importation of ideas and institutions took place. This process opened avenues as never before for Western influence. The second half of the nineteenth century saw greatly expanding Arab interest in secular education.

EDUCATION BEFORE THE INTRODUCTION OF THE WESTERN SYSTEM

In order to understand the educational system in the Arab provinces of Syria and Lebanon when foreign missionaries began to operate in the area, it is necessary to present in brief a discussion of the educational organization at the beginning of the nineteenth century. Three important factors had influenced the educational system of the Ottoman Empire:

1. The *Millet*, or religious communities system: an Ottoman political tradition according to which every millet should provide schools, headed by spiritual leaders, for its own communicants. Missionaries who went to the Arab provinces of Syria and Lebanon in the early nineteenth century created their own confessional institutions. They ignored Ottoman structures.
2. Privileges system: under this system, foreigners were allowed to build educational institutions and to undertake missionary work among non-Muslims in the Ottoman Empire, including the Arab provinces.
3. The rejection by the learned men of Islam, the *Ulama*, of any change in the traditional system of education, and their resistance to all innovations; in the Arab provinces the school system consisted of the *kuttab*, schools usually maintained in towns and villages, and the *madrasah*, schools existing only in the cities. Both systems provided elementary classes. The higher educational institutions were al-Azhar in Egypt (the leading centre of Islamic

education in the whole Islamic world), the Zaytunah in Tunis, and the Shiite college of al-Najaf in Iraq.[3] Religious educational institutions fell under an independent system and were headed by the Ulama. None of these schools restricted admissions and none required final examinations.

Egypt entered the nineteenth century with a French occupation that had created the Institut d'Egypt in 1798, but educational institutions had been founded in Egypt a long time before the arrival of the French. Jurji Zaydan, a well-known Arab historian, mentioned more than 72 schools in existence in Egypt at the turn of the nineteenth century. Their curricula included Quranic and linguistic subjects as well as medicine.[4] Abd al-Latif Tibawi, another well-known historian, asserted that al-Azhar had at the time of the French invasion 50 senior teachers (apart from many junior assistants), and more than 3000 students.[5] Tibawi has indicated how al-Azhar taught mathematics, astronomy, geography and medicine in addition to linguistic and Quranic studies.[6] James Heyworth-Dunne mentioned the names and publications of Egyptians in mathematics, astronomy and topography before the French invasion.[7] Arab educational institutions were certainly not advanced in comparison to Western ones, but there was indeed a tradition in education before the transfer of Western models to the Arab world.

Syria also had a tradition of educational institutions before the arrival of the missionaries. The largest among the kuttab and madrasah schools was al-Umawi in Damascus among at least 14 others. One of these was Ayn Waraqah, founded in 1789, which had Butrus al-Bustani, an important Arab intellectual, as a graduate.[8] Christians of all sects, Maronities, Melkites (Catholics), Orthodox and Jews also had their own school systems. Muslim Shiite schools had students from Iraq and Iran.

EDUCATIONAL CHANGE AFTER THE INTRODUCTION OF WESTERN MODELS

The first plans for modernizing educational and scientific institutions in the Arab provinces were launched in the nineteenth century as a consequence of the French occupation of Egypt in 1798.[9] The agent of change was Muhammad Ali of Egypt. When he came to power in 1805, Muhammed Ali adopted a French model and founded medical, engineering and language schools. All the schools that Ali founded were geared to military purposes and were not purely for the intellectual training of young Egyptians. Teaching was mainly in Arabic, and the language-school graduates were assigned for translation and administrative work. In 1821, Bulaq press in Cairo was inaugurated, and between 1821 and 1850 it issued 81 Arabic books on different aspects of science.[10] A Ministry of Education organized the newly created educational institutions.[11] Muhammed Ali sent more than 400 students to Europe to study all branches of science, including military tactics.

Translation was intense at the time of Ali. More than 200 books were translated into Arabic and Turkish from Western and Eastern languages.[12] After the death of Ali in 1849, this scientific movement came to a halt. Many schools were closed under the rule of Khedive Abbas and Khedive Said, including the language school. Scientific development resumed under the rule of Khedive Ismail in 1863, and a number of the suppressed schools were reopened. Ismail followed Ali's example and sent 120 more students to France to study sciences.[13]

Four factors governed educational change in Syria. The first factor was Egyptian rule over Syria and Lebanon from 1831 to 1841. The Egyptians brought with them a number of reforms. Ibrahim Pasha, the son of Muhammed Ali, required officers and soldiers to learn geometry and mathematics and provided a monthly salary for every son of a military man who joined the schools. He encouraged the publication of Arabic books which had been in meagre supply, especially those in mathematics, algebra, geometry and the natural sciences. He introduced a tolerant policy towards foreigners and local Christians that resulted in the opening of missionary schools in various parts of Syria.[14]

A second factor was the spread of printing presses and the introduction of modern educational materials. In 1727, a printing press arrived in Istanbul after stiff resistance from the *Ulama* who argued that the Word of God should be handwritten. The first Arabic press came to the Fertile Crescent in 1733, through the efforts of a Uinate Catholic Deacon, Abdallah Zakhir, in al-Shuwayr, Lebanon. He turned out religious material in Arabic. Egypt acquired its first printing press in 1821. Another Western printing press was introduced by American Protestant missionaries, who transferred their operation from Malta to Beirut in 1834. It was followed by a Jesuit press in 1847. By 1875 there were eleven printing presses in Beirut alone, four in Damascus, and three in Aleppo. Educational materials gradually made their appearance in a variety of fields such as natural sciences, the arts, literature, history and technology. Arabic transla-tion followed the publication of many European scientific texts in medicine, chemistry, pathology, physiology, and philosophy.[15]

A third factor promoting change in education in Syria is found in the Ottoman Reform laws of 1846 and 1869. While it took time before these reforms were effectively implemented in Lebanon and Syria, the laws involved a new system of elementary, secondary and higher education with new curricula. The government removed the schools from the supervision of local religious communities and opened them to all children, irrespective of their religion. The laws of 1869 provided for a minimum compulsory schooling of four years, starting at the age of seven. Most importantly, the new schools taught mathematics, history, geography and hygiene, in addition to tra-ditional subjects. At the secondary level, physics, chemistry and biol-ogy were also introduced.[16] The fourth factor encouraging change was the educational activity of Western missionaries, which will be discussed in a later section.

Under Khedive Ismail and Sultan Abd al-Aziz of the Ottoman Empire, a period of press freedom took place.[17] This freedom led to an exponential growth in the number of periodicals and scientific journals. In Beirut alone, seven new periodicals were founded in 1870. Further-more, the first scientific journals *Yacoup al-Tib* (a medical periodical) and *al-Muqtataf* were established in Cairo and Beirut in 1865 and 1876. Other scientific periodicals were also founded, mainly in Egypt and Syria. This growth was not confined to the Arab lands. Arab thinkers founded Arabic journals in Europe and North and South America. Between 1870 and 1892, for example, there were 18 in Paris and 8 in London. Even Montreal, at the turn of the century, had four periodicals and two newpapers in Arabic.[18]

The language of instruction at schools had an impact on Arab scientific development. Egyptian schools switched to English in 1887, following the British occupation. This change followed the idea that work published in English was easier to find and better in style. In Beirut, the Syrian Protestant College (SPC) also began teaching in English in 1882, after almost 16 years of instruction in Arabic. The French Jesuit university in Beirut, founded in 1875, never taught in Arabic.

These developments threw up barriers to the development of Arab science. Zaydan has emphasized:

Those who served the Arabic language in their publications, writing and scientific activities, in Syria were mostly graduated from national schools or from the Syrian Protestant College before it switched to English.[19]

Two prominent educators who dominated Arab intellectual life of the nineteenth century were Butrus al-Bustani and Rifat al-Tahtawi. Al-Bustani, a Christian Arab, was born in Lebanon in 1819. He studied at the Monastic College of Ayn Waraqah where he learned Syriac, Latin, Arabic and Canonical Law.[20] His first encounter with American missionaries took place in 1840, when he met Dr Cornelius van Dyck, a founder of the Syrian Protestant College. Al-Bustani taught at the SPC and wrote textbooks on physical science, grammar and arithmetic. He also collaborated with Eli Smith, an American missionary, in the translation of the Bible, which gave to the Arab population direct access to the Scriptures for the first time. In 1863 he established the first national school in Lebanon, following the Western model. In 1876 he published a seven-volume encyclopedia, *Dairat al-Maarif*, on modern knowledge. This work represents the highest achievement of the Arab renaissance during the last quarter of the nineteenth century. This scientific undertaking, initiated in Lebanon and Syria by al-Bustani and other Christian intellectuals like Nasif al-Yaziji, became available to other Arab provinces like Egypt.

The second great educator was Rifaa al-Tahtawi, who was born in 1801 in Egypt and educated in France.[21] After his return from Europe, he wrote many books, the most important of which is *Takhlis al-Ibriz ila Talkhis Bariz*. In his work, he provided the first modern Arabic definition of science as being 'knowledge achieved by way of evidence and proof'.[22] Tahtawi also introduced and explained many other concepts, such as the meaning of the doctrine of the modern state and the French Declaration of the Rights of Man.

MISSIONARY ZEAL AND SCIENTIFIC DEVELOPMENT: PROTESTANT VERSUS CATHOLIC

In mid-nineteenth-century Syria, fierce competition erupted between two rival missionary groups: the American Protestants and the French Jesuits. The rivalry sparked the creation of the first Western scientific institutions in the Arab World: the Syrian Protestant College and the Jesuit St Joseph's College, both in Beirut.[23]

Western Catholic missionaries had been in Syria during the seventeenth century, but their work was confined to a limited number of schools. By the time of its suppression, the Society of Jesus had achieved some gains. Not until the Egyptian occupation of Syria in 1831, and after the lifting of the ban, did the Jesuits return to Syria. As the Pope's 'shock troops', they came to counter the arrival of American Protestants.[24]

The Boston-based American Board of Commissioners for Foreign Missions had sent a mission to Syria in 1820 to carry out evangelical activity. They had first founded a mission in Malta and later moved to Beirut, where there was no native Protestant community to work with. This meant that they had to convert members of other Christian groups. The process of conversion triggered hostility between different religious denominations and almost resulted in an end to the Protestant mission in 1842.

Even though Catholic missionaries had a long lead in founding schools in different parts of Syria and Lebanon, they failed to teach in Arabic. But as soon as the Jesuits returned to Syria in 1831 and encountered their traditional competitor expanding outside of Beirut, they began to emphasize the Arabic language. This revival no doubt enhanced the spread of knowledge among the Christian Arabs.[25]

From the year 1831 onward, the spread of Jesuit secondary and higher education institutions progressed by leaps and bounds. They established a college for secondary education at the village of Ghazir, in 1843, where they introduced modern studies such as mathematics and history, in addition to theology, Arabic, Latin, Italian and French. They also revived the Ayntura College, which played an important role in the formation of native scholars.

Ghazir College continued to be the only Jesuit College for higher education until 1874 when the Jesuits created the St Joseph University. Again, the SPC was the real reason behind the foundation of the Jesuit university. Xavier Gautrelet, President of the Jesuit Society for 1875, lamented:

> What can be done? The natural place for this institution (Ghazir) is Beirut, because the American Protestants have an institution which teaches medicine, theology, and it is urgent to have a similar institution.[26]

In 1881, only six years after the creation of the University of St Joseph, the government of France certified it to grant the degrees of *baccalauréat, licence* and *doctorat.* The School of Medicine and the School of Pharmacy were established in 1883 and 1889 respectively.

The education of women also benefited from the competition between Protestants and Jesuits. Catholic schools for women were founded only after the Protestant missionary Eli Smith and his wife opened the doors of the Women's College in 1860. A school for girls was also founded by Arab nationals. The first, *Zahrat al-Ihsan*, was founded by an Arab woman, Labibah Jahshan, and financed by another Arab woman, Amali Sursuq, in 1880.

CHANNELS OF TRANSMISSION: NATIVIST VERSUS FOREIGN

The sources for modern Arab scientific development are still a matter of controversy. One view has tended to focus on the emergence and spread of Western science in the missionaries' colleges, especially the Syrian Protestant College (SPC).[27] Another view, while recognizing the value of the contributions of this college, has categorically denied such a role. Abd al-Latif Tibawi asserts that the SPC had strictly evangelical aims, and non-sectarian education was promoted by Arab nationals, like Butrus al-Bustani, who opened his National School to all creeds.[28]

Kamal al-Yaziji, professor of Arabic Literature at the American University of Beirut, argues against the views propagated by the missionary enthusiasts. He attributes nineteenth-century Arab scientific development to the intellectual stimulus that came from the West, coupled with a primitive intellectual energy in the East.[29] In his view, Western institutions supplied the Arab mind with knowledge. The evidence he provides is that, among others, Nasif al-Yaziji, a well-known man of letters, Butrus al-Bustani, and Yusuf al-Asir, a prominent Arab thinker, did not grow under the protection of missionaries.[30] Indeed, the scientific movement in Egypt started almost fifty years before the creation of foreign educational institutions. It included opening Schools of Medicine, the House of Languages and engineering studies all at the time of Muhammad Ali.[31]

At the same time, books were translated, predominantly from French, and printed in Cairo before the appearance of the missionary presses. Some were on natural philosophy, as well as mathematics, physics, chemistry, geology and the social sciences. Clot Bey, an instructor at the Egyptian School of Medicine, of French origin and a prominent figure in Egyptian scientific development, wrote a book on natural philosophy (translated into Arabic in 1838) which, sources indicate, discussed Buffon's and Lamarck's naturalist philosophy. Other books translated into Arabic in the same period were Nérée Boubée's geology, Perron's physics, Dumas' chemistry, and Girard's domestical animal sciences.[32]

Although one can find scientific writers who had no connection with the missionary schools, it is undeniable that, at both institutions, many secular subjects were introduced, including the exact and applied sciences. By 1900, 329 students had graduated from the SPC, 175 in medicine, 68 in pharmacy, and 86 in other scientific fields. Another 500 students graduated from the Jesuit university, including 120 medical doctors. Arabs who studied at each institution held important positions in Egypt and Syria.[33]

As to the scientific value of missionary education, Sarruf, one of the SPC graduates, correctly pointed out that the emphasis

> was known to be for the interest of theology, linguistics and literature. Syrians had not the opportunity to advance in natural sciences, except when students sought that knowledge in Rome, or in the medical school in Egypt.[34]

Yet staff in the early years of the SPC were very active in promoting modern science among the Arab population, and they published many books and articles on secular subjects in Arabic. Among the most active was Cornelius van Dyck, who wrote *Usul al-Kimya* (Introduction to Chemistry) in 1869 and *al-Naqsh fi al-Hajar* (On Physics, Chemistry and Geography) in 1887, he issued other books on astronomy, geometry, algebra and internal pathology. In addition to his work, he translated the New Testament into Arabic from Greek.[35] William van Dyck, third son of Cornelius van Dyck, joined the teaching staff of the SPC in 1880. He authored a paper on street dogs in Beirut which he sent to Darwin, who wrote a preface for it in 1882. The paper was published in the proceedings of the British Zoological Society in 1882.[36] George Post published *Nizam al-Halaqat fi Silsilat Dhawat al-Faqrat* (On the System of the Chain of the Vertebrates) in 1869, *Mabadi Ilm al-Nabat* (Fundamentals of Botany) in 1871 and *Flora of Syria, Palestine and Sinai* in 1883.[37]

The scientific value of these and other publications of professors at the SPC is at best modest. Scrutiny of the work of professors of mathematics and astronomy from 1866 to 1930, with the help of Poggendorff's bio-bibliography, suggests only a small contribution to knowledge.[38] Perhaps the most talented researcher at the SPC was Raymond Dugan, although his scientific work was carried out under the supervision of Max Wolf, a German astronomer.[39] From this point of view, there seems much of value in Tibawi's assessment that the SPC did not provide a direct channel for allowing Western science to take root on Arab land.

THE FOUNDATION OF ARAB LEARNED SOCIETIES

This history of the early Arab learned societies is impressive when we consider the prevailing political conditions of Ottoman despotism. The earliest society emerged during the first half of the nineteenth century, at about the same time that a new wave of European scientific societies were created.

George Antonius has remarked that it was al-Bustani and al-Yaziji who, after consultation with the Americans, suggested the foundation of the Society of Arts and Science in Beirut.

> Due to the spread of education in the schools and the birth of a new interest in the sciences, some effort ought to be made to promote knowledge among adults by bringing them into touch with Western cultures.[40]

Noted Arabs among the members of the society were al-Yaziji and al-Bustani, as well as Eli Smith, Cornelius van Dyck and other Americans. Even though the membership of the society reached 50 in two years, not a single Muslim was present. The society had a modest library. According to Eli Smith's report to the *German Journal of the Asiatic Society* in 1847, the library had 756 books, 527 in Arabic and Turkish and 229 in other languages. Of these, 242 books were donated and the rest, 514 books, were bought by a Lebanese national, N. Thabit, for 7000 piastres. Although most of the books were on religious and linguistic subjects 24 treated medicine, 9 mathematics and geometry and 8 astronomy. Meetings were conducted in Arabic at least once a month with discussion mainly on scientific subjects. Most contributors were Arabs. For example, Salem Nofal discussed natural laws, Cornelius van Dyck science and its fruits, Nofal N. Nofal plants (botany), Yuhanna Wortabat modern science in Syria, Nasif al-Yaziji Arab sciences and Butrus al-Bustani women's education. The society lasted a mere five years, and its proceedings were published by al-Bustani in 1852.[41]

The Jesuits followed the Protestant example and founded the Oriental Society in 1850 at the initiative of the French priest Deprunières (1821–1872). In organization it followed the Society of Arts and Sciences. Its members were exclusively Christian, either Arabs or foreigners. According to Yusuf Sarkis, the Oriental Society was both literary and scientific. The record of the first meeting was written in an awkward, unclear Arabic. The subjects of discussion ranged widely. For example, Daoud Bertrand delivered a speech on astronomy, Dr Sokah spoke in French and N. Gigano gave the translation. The president of this society was a Frenchman and his assistant was M. Naqqash, a native Arab. The organization expired after only two years.[42]

The short life of these societies was due in some measure to Ottoman control over the press, although both were perceived as foreign intrusions. In 1857, the Syrian Scientific Society emerged from the ashes of its two predecessors. It differed from both the Oriental and Arts and Science societies in that its members were all Arabs, Muslims as well as Christians. Membership rose to more than 150 and included leading Arab dignitaries of all religions.[43] The civil war in Lebanon of 1860 produced a temporary setback for this society, and in 1868 it was reconstituted. The new president was a Muslim, Amir Muhammad Bin Amin Arslan. His constituency came from all over the Arab world and Turkey, and it included a number of foreign consuls. Discussions at the meetings of the society included the needs of the intellect, the life of Aristotle, agriculture, the history of European civilization, medicine, physical sciences, solar photography, the function of bodily organs, the status of education, the need for civilization and the history of Syria. The society published a monthly journal, *Majmuat al-Ulum* (The Sum of Sciences). It survived barely more than a year.

In 1882 the Syrian Scientific Society reopened for the third time under the name Eastern Scientific Society. Its goal was the advancement of applied science, for example, meteorological forecasts. Its members were both Christians and Muslims. *Al-Muqtataf* reported some of the proceedings of the society. These featured, among other things, astronomy, botany, engineering and mathematical topics. The society disappeared after Nimr and Sarruf, prominent members, left for Egypt in 1884.[44]

Another industrial society was established by Shahin Makarius in Beirut in 1883, it was called al-Jamaya al-Sinaiya.[45] Some of its proceedings were reported in *al-Muqtataf* in 1883. At one meeting, an unknown member of the society discussed methods for producing local ink for printing which could substitute for the imported product.[46] Still another learned society called Shams al-Birr (The Sun of Charity) was founded in 1869. Although the society was labelled philanthropic, *al-Muqtataf* reported on two of its meetings in 1883 where Nimr discussed materialism, and Wortabat talked about life from birth to death.[47] Other societies mentioned by historians include 'Zahrat al-Adab' and 'Zahrat al-Ihsan', founded in 1873 and 1880, but no indication survives of their scientific activities.[48] Whatever the final assessment of these ephemeral organizations, they clearly demonstrate the Arab effort to study and apply modern science.

Egyptian learned societies were also active, although they operated for the most part in the shadow of imperialist armies. It was Napoleon who founded the first learned society in Egypt, l'Institut de l'Egypt, in 1798.[49] It expired after Napoleon's forces departed, but revived in 1869 under the waning sun of the Second French Empire, retaining its French character throughout the subsequent British occupation. Its publications concerned engineering, medical and agricultural subjects. From 1880 to 1885 the Egyptian Scientific Society published six volumes on Egyptian archaeology, geology and botany.[50] The Egyptian Scientific Society was followed by a number of other associations such as the Geographical Society founded in 1875, and the Agricultural Society founded in 1898.[51]

ARAB SCIENTIFIC JOURNALISM

Three Arab scientific journals form the basis of discussion in many of the following pages: *al-Muqtataf, al-Hilal* and *al-Mashriq*.[52] The importance of Arab periodicals stems from the fact that they circulated before the appearance of modern Arab universities and specialized education. When scientific books were not easily available, Arabic periodicals, scientific or literary, were the main vehicles for propagating modern thought.[53] The first modern periodical appeared in Egypt in 1828 and was called *al-Waqai*. It was followed by *Hadiqat al-Akhbar* (The Garden of News) in Beirut, published by K. al-Khuri in 1857.[54] Under the liberal rule of Khedive Ismail and Sultan Abd al-Aziz in the 1870's many journals and papers appeared. The first Arab scientific periodical was *Yacoub al-Tib* (Medical Review), which appeared in Egypt in 1865. It discussed only medical matters that had direct bearing on Egyptian health problems, and no philosophical questions were mentioned. While the total number of periodicals in Arabic exceeded 3200 for the period 1800 to 1929, the vast majority were short lived.[55]

The most important of Arab scientific reviews was *al-Muqtataf*. It was founded in Beirut by Sarruf and Nimr in 1876, and moved to Egypt in 1885. From 1927, after Sarruf's death, it was continued by his nephew Fuad until 1944. The review lasted until 1952. The American University of Beirut provided a three-volume index to the journal in 1967. *Al-Muqtataf*, a monthly review, was the main channel for transmitting new ideas about the technical aspects of scientific civilization to the Arab world.[56]

The role of *al-Muqtataf* in adapting science to Arab needs has been recognized by both Arab and non-Arab sources. Al-Zahawi for example praised its role in adapting science to the Arab language by providing new scientific terms.[57] An American commentator's view, published in 1882, is the generally accepted one today:

> The Muktataf, an enterprising and ably conducted scientific Magazine, is highly valued among the Arab students of the Levant and is the medium of communication between the best scientific thought of our times, as it appears in the European and American Journals and the awakening mind of the Arabic-speaking East. It also contains earnest and thoughtful original discussions of current topics, and much practical information adapted to local needs. Its mission is a stimulating and timely one among the educated classes in Syria and Egypt.[58]

While the editors of *al-Muqtataf* and those who wrote in it were predominantly Christians, they nevertheless managed to identify themselves with the Muslim community by urging all Arabs to follow the example of Western civilization. Arabs could progress, they argued, if they adopted the proper methods of education. Arab writers in *al-Muqtataf* linked the idea of progress with that of evolution. It is no surprise, therefore, to find that *al-Muqtataf* devoted much of its discussion to different aspects of Darwinism.

Al-Hilal (The Crescent) was the second influential periodical of the time. It was founded by Jurji Zaydan (1861–1914), a Lebanese Christian, in Cairo in 1892.[59] He edited his journal until his death, when his son Emil succeeded to the task. The journal is still published in Cairo. In its early years, *al-Hilal* focused on historical matters, ranging from writing on Western civilization to the history of science, literature, and Islam. The journal reflected Zaydan's own interests. He published five volumes on the history of Islamic civilization, a history of the Arabs before Islam and a history of Arabic literature.[60] He also wrote twenty-one historical novels. He was convinced that Arab backwardness could be alleviated by adopting Western science.

Al-Mashriq was the third major journal launched by an Arab Christian. It began in 1898 and lasted until 1971. The founding editor was Father Louis Cheikho, S.J. While the journal dealt with science, literature and the arts, its true nature was religious. We find the expected debate between *al-Mashriq*, on the one hand, and *al-Muqtataf* and *al-Hilal*, on the other hand, regarding different aspects of the relationship between science and religion.

Al-Mashriq published many articles that tackled scientific issues, especially Darwinism, on religious grounds. Apart from Cheikho's contributions, the journal featured other writers – Christians, Muslims, and Orientalists – who wrote on contemporary issues. Unlike liberal Arab journals, *al-Mashriq* mentioned Islamic publications on traditional questions. In fact, it praised the publications of Isfahani and Afghani on the theory of evolution. This is in sharp contrast to *al-Muqtataf* and *al-Hilal*, which did not mention these authors.

ARAB SCIENTIFIC WRITERS: A PERSONAL VIEW

The aim of this section is to introduce Arab authors or editors whose work is discussed in the following study. The figures are Jamal al-Din al-Afghani (1839-1897), Hussein al-Jisr (1845–1909), Yaqub Sarruf (1852–1927), Shibli Shumayyil (1853–1917), Louis Cheikho (1859–1928), Salama Musa (1887–1958), Ismail Mazhar (1891–1962), Abu al-Faraj Muhammad Rida al-Isfahani, Mustafa al-Mansuri, and Hasan Hussein.[61]

Jamal al-Din al-Afghani

Al-Afghani was born in Asadabad, Persia. In Kabul he received a broad Islamic education and showed interest in philosophy and science. As a young man, he served as minister to a contender for the throne of Kabul, a contender who was ultimately defeated by a rival. Soon after the failure of his political ambitions in 1870, Afghani went to India and Egypt. Then he travelled to Istanbul, where he was soon expelled on the accusation of teaching heretical philosophy. He stayed in Egypt until his expulsion in 1879, by Khediva Tawfiq. During the Egyptian period, he exerted a great influence in intellectual circles.[62] One of his followers, Muhammad Abduh, followed Afghani to Paris, where they published an influential Arabic periodical, *Al-Urwa al-Wuthqa* (The Indissoluble Link). It lasted six months. While in Paris, Afghani battled with Ernest Renan on the question of Islam and science in the pages of the *Journal des débats*. In 1885, he visited London on the invitation of W.S. Blunt to discuss the political future of Egypt and Sudan.[63]

Afghani had a great impact not only on the Arab world, but also on the whole Muslim East. He was the first to introduce the notion of a 'Pan-Islamic movement' late in the nineteenth century. Here, we are mainly concerned with his reaction to Darwinism and materialism and not his political activities. In 1881 Afghani published a text *The Refutation of Materialism* (Al-Radd ala al-Dahriyyin), in Persian.[64] It was translated into Arabic by Abduh. In his *Refutation*, he attacked the materialists (*naycheris*) and defended Islam as the greatest of all religions. Obviously, the first part, dealing with Darwin's theory of evolution and materialism, will be the subject of our analysis.

When one speaks of Afghani's work, a brief introduction to Muhammad Abduh (1849–1905), his disciple, is essential.[65] Abduh was born in Tanta, Egypt. He attended traditional school and later went to al-Azhar for higher studies. Upon graduation, he was appointed a teacher at al-Azhar. During Afghani's stay in Egypt in 1871, Abduh was his closest companion. He was soon influenced by Afghani's interpretation of Islam to suit the modern age of science. In this respect, Abduh attempted to use modern terms to defend Islamic values. His writing on the compatibility of Islam with modern realities proved to be influential on the public mind and the next generation of Arab thinkers.[66] Following his expulsion by the British authorities for his political activities, he lived in Beirut and Paris where he joined Afghani in founding the periodical, *al-Urwa al-Wuthqa*.

The main focus of Abduh's ideas was the relationship between science and religion, as he held that there was no contradiction between Islam and reason, or between Quranic teaching and science. For him, Islam encouraged rational thinking and discouraged blind imitation. He attacked fatalism and promoted the idea of free will. Abduh, who later in his life was appointed the *Mufti* of Egypt, the highest possible religious position, opened the doors for *ijtihad* (interpretation of the Quran in the light of modern developments). While this interpretation aimed to limit the spread of secularism, as Hourani has argued, Abduh's notion was used by Arab secularists to gain more ground.[67]

Hussein al-Jisr (1845–1909)

A shaykh of Muslim Shiite faith, al-Jisr was born in Tripoli, Lebanon, and had a private education.[68] His father died when he was a child. Later, he studied traditional education in Arabic grammar and Quranic studies at al-Azhar. In 1867, back in Lebanon, he taught and published. Many Arab scholars studied under his supervision, for example Rashid Rida, editor of *al-Manar*, a monthly journal, and Abd al-Qadir al-Moghribi, a member of the Arab Learned Society (al-Majma al-Ilmi al-Arabi) of Damascus. His son, Muhammad was the chief parliamentarian of Lebanon. Al-Jisr was the president of Jamiyyat al-Maqasid al-Islamiyya (The Arab Charitable Organization) in Beirut.[69]

Al-Jisr edited *Jaridat Tarablus* (The Tripoli Newspaper).[70] He wrote more than 25 books on different aspects of Islamic religion, among the most important was his long book, *Al-Risalah al-Hamidiyya fi Haqiqat al-Dianah al-Islamiyya wa-Haqiqat al-Shariah al-Muhammadiyya* (A Hamedian Essay on the Truthfulness of Islamic Religion and the Truthfulness of Muhammadan Canon Laws). It appeared in Beirut in 1887. Its aim was to present Islam in a new way in order to accommodate the new scientific development of the age.[71] Therefore, in his refutation of materialism and Darwinism, he insisted on reason and the empirical interpretation of the Quran. This rationalistic study of Islam helped al-Jisr to win a prize from Sultan Abd al-Hamid.

Yaqub Sarruf (1852–1927)

Sarruf was born in Al-Hadath, Lebanon, in 1852 and died in Cairo in 1927.[72] A Catholic, he was among the first group who graduated from the Syrian Protestant College in 1870. After graduation, he taught in many Lebanese schools. Later in his life, he converted to Protestanism.

In 1876, he and Faris Nimr, another graduate from the SPC, founded and edited one of the earliest scientific periodicals in the Arab World, *al-Muqtataf* (Choice Selections). Sarruf taught at the SPC from 1873 until his departure to Egypt in 1884. His journal continued its distinguished career after it moved to Cairo, ceasing publication only in 1952. Sarruf was also co-editor with Nimr of *al-Muqattam* newspaper, founded in 1889. It had the largest circulation of any Arabic newspaper.

Sarruf's effort to adapt Arabic to the modern sciences was immense. In his writings on chemistry, biology, astronomy and mathematics, he introduced terms which enriched the Arabic language with modern concepts.[73] More than an editor, Sarruf was the author of several books on scientific and literary matters. Most important were *Wassail Ilm al-Falak* (Means of Astronomy) and *Usul Ilm al-Kimya* (Principles of Chemistry).[74] In 1883, both Nimr and Sarruf resigned from the SPC, probably as a result of their indirect support of Darwin's ideas. The introduction of those ideas by Edwin Lewis, an American professor, resulted in a much studied crisis which erupted in 1882. As a result, both Sarruf and Nimr left for Egypt.

When we discuss Sarruf's scientific life, a brief discussion of Nimr is essential.[75] Nimr was born at Hasbayya, Lebanon, in 1856, and died in Cairo in 1952. After his father's death in the civil war of 1860, he accompanied his mother to Jerusalem and later to Beirut, where he attended missionary schools. He graduated from the SPC in 1874 and was appointed by the same college as instructor in astronomy. From 1876 to 1889, Nimr co-edited *al-Muqtataf* and in 1889, he became the editor of *al-Muqattam*, a joint project with Sarruf. Nimr was nominated a member in the British Philosophical Society in 1887, and in the same year, he also received the Order of Golden Education from King Oscar of Sweden, for his contribution to educational development in the Arab world.

In 1890, both Sarruf and Nimr were awarded honorary doctorates by New York University to honour their work on their scientific journal.[76] During his intellectual life, Nimr produced articles on astronomy and translated Edwin Lewis' book on meteorology, *Al-Zawahir al-Jawwiyah* (The Principles of Meteorology), in 1876. In 1882, Nimr, Sarruf and other Arab scholars created the Eastern Scientific Society 'al-Majma al-Ilmi al-Sharqi'. It disappeared after their departure to Egypt in 1884.

Shibli Shumayyil (1853–1917)

Shumayyil was born in Kafr Shima, Lebanon.[77] He grew up in an intellectual environment. His elder brother Milhim, a teacher at one of the Orthodox schools in Beirut, also wrote on various philosophical themes. His other brother, Amin, published a law journal.[78] Thus, Shumayyil's family stimulated his intellect appetite. A Uinate Catholic by birth, he studied medicine at the Syrian Protestant College. He was among the first graduating class in 1871.[79] He spent a year in Paris before settling in Egypt, where he practised his profession in the town of Tanta. As a physician, Shumayyil practised surgery, obstetrics, dentistry and other medical skills. This was simply due to the lack of specialization in medicine at that period.

From 1886 to 1891, he published *al-Shifa* (Healing), a monthly periodical in medicine and surgery.[80] He contributed scores of articles to different journals, especially *al-Muqtataf*,[81] on a wide variety of subjects, most importantly the theory of evolution and materialism. Most of his articles were collected and published in two volumes in 1910. The first volume was entitled *Falsafat al-Nushu wa al-Irtiqa* (The Philosophy of Evolution and Progress). The second volume bore the title *Majmuat al-Doctor Shibli Shumayyil* (Collected Writings of Doctor Shibli Shumayyil). He also translated and edited several books, including Ludwig Büchner's *Commentary on Darwin*,[82] the Tracts of Epicurus, and Avicenna's *Verses*. He published *Tarikh al-Tibb* (History of Medicine) in 1879.[83]

Shumayyil was an ardent advocate of materialism and evolution, and he was for many years the only thinker, and perhaps the first of his time, to discuss materialistic thought in the Arab world.

Louis Cheikho (1859–1928)

Cheikho was born in Mardin, Syria.[84] A Uinate Catholic, he studied at Ghazir, a Jesuit school. Later he went to France and other European countries where he studied theology, philosophy and languages and acquainted himself with the Western method of research and publication. Back in Beirut, he was appointed professor of Arabic at the Jesuit St Joseph's College.

In 1898, he launched and edited *al-Mashriq*, a monthly periodical on literature, science and history. He also established the 'Oriental Library' (al-Maqtabah al-Sharqiyyah) at the Jesuit university.[85] This library became a respected centre of scholarly research. Cheikho wrote more than fifty books on historical and literary subjects in addition to numerous articles in his journal.[86] He also attended some of the Orientalists' conferences that were held in Europe at that time.

Cheikho was notable in his defence of the Catholic religion against all comers. He spared no effort to attack bitterly Darwin's ideas and those who popularized them in the Arab world, at least those who did so on purely religious grounds. His ardent support of Catholicism brought him into conflict with both Christians and Muslims. Muhammad Kurd Ali, a Muslim, and Sarruf, a Christian, each accused him of racial and religious discrimination. It is important to note that Cheikho never attacked Sumayyil's materialistic ideas, no doubt because Shumayyil was Catholic.[87]

Salama Musa (1887–1958)

Musa was born in Egypt in 1887. A Christian Copt who attended a Coptic primary school, he went to Cairo for his secondary education. His father, a civil servant, died when Musa was two years old. Unlike other Arab thinkers, he took the unusual step of publishing his autobiography, *Tarbiyat Salama Musa* (The Education of Salama Musa).[88] Musa visited Paris in 1907, at the age of nineteen, and attended courses in law and literature at the Paris faculties. In 1909 he moved to London, where he spent four years. He joined the socialist Fabian Society and became well acquainted with the ideas of H. G. Wells and George Bernard Shaw.[89] Later, he turned to Marx, Goethe, Freud and Spencer.

In Egypt, Musa published the short-lived weekly journal *al-Mustaqbal* (The Future). He put his experience with Western thought into articles published in Egyptian periodicals, among them *al-Muqtataf,* and *al-Hilal.* In 1929 he also launched another periodical called *al-Majalla al-Jadida* (The New Journal), a monthly review that went on a sporadically until 1942.

Musa was a prolific writer.[90] His entire intellectual output is beyond the scope of this work, although it is well to emphasize that in most of his publications he referred to Darwin's theory in one way or another.

The writings of Musa analyzed in my study include *Muqadimat al-Superman* (The Advent of the Superman), his first essay, published in 1909; *Mukhtarat Salama Musa* (Selections from Salama

Musa) in 1926, *Al-Yawn wa-al-Ghadd* (Today and Tomorrow) in 1927, *Nazariyat al-Tatawwur wa Asl al-Insan* (Theory of Evolution and the Origin of Man) in 1928 and articles written on different aspects of Western science in his journal and other periodicals. Musa's last work was also on evolution, entitled *Al-Insan Qimmat al-Tatawwur* (Man is the Acme of Evolution), appearing in 1961. In all his work, he was directed by modern science and retained a deep aversion to religion.[91]

Ismail Mazhar (1891–1962)

Mazhar was born in Egypt into a well-to-do Muslim family.[92] His father and grandfather were engineers. His father participated with a French engineer in building several of Cairo's bridges.[93] He attended the elite Nasiriyyah school and later studied at al-Khediwi school, where he completed his secondary education. Unlike Shumayyil and Sarruf, he did not attend an institution of higher education, except for brief literary and Arabic courses at al-Azhar. He belonged to Musa's generation, and his career lasted until 1962.

Mazhar was a prolific writer, editor, journalist, and translator. He published various studies on history and scientific literature totalling more than twenty books. He also published almost four years of a monthly journal *al-Usur* (Centuries) of which he wrote the major part himself.[94] He also edited *al-Muqtataf* for a short period beginning in 1945.[95]

In 1909, while a student, he published *al-Shaab* (The People), a scientific and educational periodical. He also launched another journal in September 1927, *al-Usur*, a controversial monthly which was discontinued in July 1930. He contributed many articles to *al-Muqtataf*, *al-Liwa* and Al-Kitab al-Sanawi Li al-Majma al-Misri Li al-Thaqafa al-Ilmiyya (The Egyptian Society for Scientific Culture).

The works of Mazhar considered in my study include his 1918 translation of Darwin's *The Origin of Species*. He was the first Arab writer to translate the work. In 1926 he published *Malqa al-Sabil fi Madhhab al-Nushu wa al-Irtiqa* (On the Theory of Evolution and Progress) which contained a response to Shumayyil's materialism, al-Afghani's work on the *Refutation of Materialists,* and other relevant articles published in *al-Muqtataf* and *al-Usur* on Darwinism. He was, of course, a devoted supporter of Darwin's theory of evolution.

Shumayyil, Musa, and to a lesser degree, Ismail Mazhar, can be considered without reservations to be the apostles of evolution to the Arab world.

2 General Remarks on the Impact of Darwinism

INTRODUCTION

A great deal of literature has appeared about Darwin and Darwinism in the Western world. Numerous books provide accounts of Darwin's life and of his theory and the role it plays in biology and the development of modern thought.[1] It seems that the Darwinian revolution (to use Kuhn's term) and the impact of Darwinism now have a secure place in the history of Western thought.

As a result of the Eurocentrism of writers on Darwinism, it is not generally recognized that a significant literature on Darwinism exists in Arabic, originating in what many commentators have identified as a backward and non-scientific society. A number of historians, both Arabs and non-Arabs, have studied Arabic history from the social, psychological, political and other points of views, but none has considered in detail the story of Darwinism, its influence and its synthesis in Arab thought.[2] Though some recognition has been given to several Arab thinkers in this period such as Shibli Shumayyil, Farah Antun, or Salama Musa, little notice has been given to them as writers on science.[3]

The introduction of Western science to the Arab world has had a deep impact on the public mind, especially when it touches on basic beliefs, values and ideas. As in the West, the theory of evolution created intense debate among Arab thinkers during the second half of the nineteenth century. The educated public was greatly concerned with the implications of the theory for their own personal standing in the ordered universe and with the possible undermining of established religious convictions. Arab intellectuals were confronted with a cluster of disputed theories on creationism, the origin of man, the biological nature of man, the mystery of life and the relation between religious and scientific truth.

Even though the aim of this study is not to trace modern Arab

22

intellectual developments, one must emphasize that the introduction of Darwinism in the 1870's came at a time when educated Arabs were being made aware of Western ideas and the spirit of reform. The influence of the thought of the French Revolution, the impact of the French invasion, the translation movement of Muhammed Ali, and the educational impact of numerous missionaries marked a new departure in the process of the Arab *Nahda* (Awakening). Consequently, the formative years of the late nineteenth century were characterized by the increasing interest in secular learning and social change. There were the years when the germs of Western scientific thought infected a new Arab intelligentsia. It was an era in which scientific, social, political and economic ideas were translated, expounded, discussed and examined. Every aspect of human endeavour was looked at from a new perspective.

In such a period, Arab interest in Darwinism centred on its philosophical, social and political implications, rather than on its status as a biological theory. Indeed, none of the learned circles at the time, foreign or national, were mature enough to elaborate on Darwinism. Yet, surprisingly enough, some Arab modernists adopted Darwin's ideas *in toto*. The result was a series of intense intellectual battles fought in the pages of Arabic periodicals and books in, and even outside of, the Arab world.

What were the reasons for these heated debates? Essentially not to clarify the development of new knowledge, although the desire to do this played a role. As in the West, Arab traditionalists found themselves exposed to a new philosophy whic'ı threatened to tear apart the fabric of society. As a consequence, a number of prominent Arab reformers, both Christian and Muslim, sponsored many themes and methods to reconcile religious values with the rising influence of scientific realities.

Darwin's theory was not only a scientific paradigm providing biologists with a set of rules to answer many of their research problems, but also went far beyond restructuring a new mode of investigation in the biological field. Transformed into a set of ideas of universal application, Darwin's theory triggered varied inquiry into many aspects of human activity. The diffusion of evolutionary theory implied that, in a number of cases, Darwin became a minor figure in the movement called Darwinism. The importance of Herbert Spencer, Ernst Haeckel and Henri Bergson in transmitting evolutionary ideas is recognized by many scholars. The application of Darwin's theory by Spencer to encompass the whole cosmos had a great impact on shaping Arab and intellectual life. A lesser known figure, Ludwig Büchner, also had a profound impact on Arab thought. This point will be elaborated upon later.

While Darwin had not attempted to explain the general laws of evolution, Darwinism has been used to denote many things to many people. The term Darwinism can indicate Darwin's specific explanation of the theory of evolution by natural selection. It can also be used in a broader sense to mean any evolutionary theory with or without natural selection which rejects Lamarck's ideas on the inheritance of acquired characteristics. Some writers have equated Darwinism with Social Darwinism. Just because the term was used in a broader context, it is hard to avoid a certain imprecision when discussing the influence of Darwinism on the Arab world. While it is true that Arab thinkers concentrated their discussion on Social Darwinism, they nevertheless referred to many other aspects of the theory.

While the idea of evolution is not a new concept in modern times, two novel views were advanced in the nineteenth century regarding it. One group of thinkers applied the idea to the whole universe, including matter and force. Another group restricted its application to the world of living organisms, including the kingdom of plants and animals and the human race. Those who adopted the general theory of evolution faced, undoubtedly, the controversial issue of creationism and the forces that control the universe. The advocates of the evolution of living things concentrated on the impact of natural factors, such as climate, environment and the availability of food, and did not elaborate beyond these matters. In so doing they avoided a direct confrontation with those who believed in extra-natural control by religious powers. Thinkers who generalized the notion of evolution to encompass the whole universe, however, needed to resolve the issue of the forces that regulate the world, and this issue could not be separated from the question of creation and creator.

Among Western intellectuals, one of the most articulate spokesmen for the general principles of evolution was Herbert Spencer (1820–1903). Before Darwin published the *Origin of Species*, Spencer had organized a general philosophical theory based on the principle of evolution. He defined the term evolution as:

An integration of matter and concomitant dissipation of motion, during which the matter passes from an indefinite incoherent homogeneity to a definite coherent heterogeneity; and during which the retained motion undergoes a parallel transformation.[4]

For him, evolution was progress, a movement from simple, undifferentiated matter to more complex, differentiated matter. He also explained that the evolution of life was a complete adaptation between the needs of a living organism and its natural environment. In other words, environment is the direct cause for variations among species. Spencer applied his principles of survival of the fittest, a *laissez-faire* social system coupled with innate struggle, in a highly formal way. In the following pages I stress the deep-rooted confusions of Spencerism, which led Arab thinkers, religious or secular, to attack his ideas on philosophical grounds.

Arab thinkers of the Middle Ages, who took the idea of evolution from the ancient Greeks, gave great consideration to the ideas of organic evolution and transformationism in the plant and animal kingdom. While the medieval Arab contribution to evolution cannot be explored here, it is sufficient to mention that Arab writings in some ways approached those of Charles Darwin.

Arab philosophers, al-Farabi, al-Kitbi, al-Qazwini, Ibn Miskewayh, and Ibn Khaldun, among others, deliberated long and hard on related subjects, and their writings remained in the background of nineteenth-century debates. Yaqub Sarruf, for example, mentioned and quoted ancient Arab thinkers, like al-Khazini and Ibn Tufayl, when he discussed Darwinism. He quoted the following from an author as an indication of ancient Arab knowledge of evolution:

> When an illiterate public hears the man of science say that gold is a material that evolves gradually towards perfection, they think that gold has to develop through the stages of being lead, tin, copper, silver and later gold. But they cannot understand that what the scientists mean is the same as when they say that man has evolved gradually into the state in which he is. They think that what the learned men are saying is that man begins by being an Ox, then develops to an Ass, then a Mare, a Monkey and eventually a Man.[5]

Even though Orientalists and historians have hardly mentioned Arab contributions to the concept of evolution, a number of influential Arab thinkers of modern times appealed to the writing of their ancestors. They denied the fact that the theory of evolution was a discovery of Darwin and Wallace.[6] Others indicated that what Darwin explained was a part of Arab elaborations on the whole notion of transmutation.[7]

In general, however, educated Arab inquiry about their ancestors' contributions to evolution subsided after 1912. As Sarruf pointed out, the idea of evolution was an ancient one, but Darwin's work put it on the solid ground of natural selection and the survival of the fittest.[8] Impatient with many questions of the same genre, Sarruf, in his rejoinders, criticized the exaggerated, and sometimes unfounded, Arab ideas on evolution.

EARLY APPEARANCE OF DARWIN'S IDEAS IN ARABIC

The appearance of Darwinism in Arabic can be attributed to Arab nationals – Christians and Muslims – as well as to pioneering missionaries of the staff of the SPC. Foreign professors like Cornelius van Dyck, his son William, and Edwin Lewis were dedicated to introducing scientific literature to the Arab world. The introduction of modern science in general and Darwinism in particular led to the emergence of two opposing groups. One, represented by the conservative elements of both Christian and Muslim scholars, considered only religious books as the basis of knowledge and saw no need to import 'corrupt' scientific ideas from the West. The central figure in this group was, undoubtedly, Louis Cheikho. The other group, also composed of Muslims and Christians, reacted positively to Western sciences and asserted that the foundation for a new civilization should be based on borrowing and adopting these sciences. This group consisted of two wings. The moderate wing was represented by, among others, Yaqub Sarruf, Faris Nimr, Jamal al-Din al-Afghani, Rashid Rida and Ismail Mazhar.[9] The radical wing included Shibli Shumayyil, Farah Antun, and Salama Musa.[10] This radical wing, under the leadership of Shumayyil, asserted that rather than religious dogmas (the cause of Arab backwardness) science should be the basis for Arab progress.

A survey of Arab literature reveals that, although the work of Darwin was discussed in the 1870s, it was not until after the crisis of 1882 had erupted at the SPC and after the French translation of Ludwig Büchner's work on Darwinism had been presented to Arab readers by Shumayyil in 1884, that the discussion became a full-fledged polemic. Although it is true that Shumayyil first heard about Darwin's creed while studying medicine at the SPC in 1871, reference to Darwin is almost non-existent in the Arab journals before 1876. The earliest discussion of Darwin's doctrine appeared in the first year of publication of *al-Muqtataf*, in 1876. This was a series of articles on the origin of man written by Rizqallah al-Barbari,[11] a Lebanese

Christian and former teacher of Sarruf's at the SPC. As will be seen in the following pages, these articles, which appeared 17 years after the publication of Darwin's *Origin* and 5 years after the appearance of the *Descent of Man*, avoided controversy in the Arab world because they contested Darwin's anti-biblical views and praised Darwin himself as a man of vision who really did not deny the existence of God.[12]

In 1882, Edwin Lewis, an American professor at the SPC delivered a speech which seemed to favour Darwinism.[13] Lewis was not a Darwinist, but the result of his speech was a crisis of great proportions.[14] Many professors resigned, including Lewis himself. This startling incident incited a debate on Darwinism in the pages of *al-Muqtataf* between Lewis, supported by Sarruf on the one side, and James Denis, an American theologian, backed by Yusuf al-Haik, an Egyptian from Alexandria, on the other side.[15] The internecine exchange lasted until 1884. During this period, Lewis returned to the United States.

In 1884, after Shumayyil visited Paris and read about Darwin's work, he published his translation of Büchner's commentary on Darwin.[16] This publication certainly transferred the intellectual battle over Darwinism from European scientific circles to the Arab world and even to the whole Muslim East.

The first Arabic translation of the first six chapters of the *Origin of Species* came in 1918, by Ismail Mazhar, an Egyptian Muslim who was an ardent supporter of Darwinism.[17] The *Descent of Man* was also translated into Arabic by Mazhar.[18] A translation of Ernst Haeckel's book on the philosophy of evolution was completed by Hasan Hussein 1924.[19]

The intellectual storm that erupted in the Arab world in particular, and the Muslim East in general, after the appearance of Shumayyil's work on Darwinism gave rise to enormous criticism from people in all walks of life. In evaluating the views presented by Arab thinkers, whether pro-Darwinist or anti-Darwinist, I distinguish between the writing of Muslims (Sunni and Shiite sects) and Christians (Protestant, Catholic and Orthodox denominations). Foreign Christians writing in Arabic on the subject will not be discussed, since they have been dealt with by other historians.[20] One of the Christian groups under study consists of Shumayyil, Sarruf and Salama Musa. All were Darwinists. A second group, headed by Father Louis Cheikho, bitterly attacked Darwin's evolution. The third group of whom I treat are the Muslims. These may be subdivided into the following:

traditionalists or religious conservatives like Hussein al-Jisr, Hasan Hussein and Rida al-Isfahani; reformists like Jamal al-Din al-Afghani; and secularists, like Ismail Mazhar and al-Mansuri.

3 Secularist Christian Responses to Darwinism: Ideas and Ideologies

INTRODUCTION

The attempt to reconcile science and religion was most difficult for Arabs attempting to recast traditional ideas in a Darwinist framework. In Cairo and Beirut, in the late nineteenth century, a remarkable group of serious thinkers turned their discussion to the study of this issue. The central spokesman for the group was Shibli al-Shumayyil. He sought to use Darwin's ideas to alleviate Arab misery and backwardness under Ottoman despotism. He and other Arab secularists, including Muslims and Christians, produced, after their own fashion, a great commitment to science and its methods of inquiry.

All Arab supporters of science assumed faith in reason. They wanted complete freedom for human investigation from the objections raised by religious men or theologians who believed in revelation and a metaphysical world. All Christians and Muslims, modernists or reformists, were uniformly critical of traditional religious groups in one way or another. While Musa and Shumayyil, both Christians, categorically denounced religious dogmas that endangered science, Sarruf, a Christian, and Mazhar, a Muslim, proclaimed allegiance to religious faith and demonstrated the compatibility between scientific knowledge and faith. They all shared a common concern with Darwinism in all its aspects: scientific, social, philosophical and moral.

This chapter discusses the ideas and ideologies of three Westernized Arab thinkers. They are Shibli Shumayyil, Salama Musa and Yaqub Sarruf. It examines one aspect of modern Arab thought, namely the emergence of scientific and Darwinian thinking. It

29

illustrates that Darwinism, as a mode of thinking, was reconstructed by scientific and secularist thinkers as a response to the introduction of Western rationality to the Arab world.

SHIBLI SHUMAYYIL

Scientific and materialist thought

Shumayyil took science to mean more than a method of thinking or reasoning. It was the path to uncovering the hidden laws of nature and even a style of worship. In his view science was a metaphysical construct, as developed by Huxley and Spencer in England, and by Haeckel and Büchner in Germany, out of the cautious hypotheses of Darwin. He based his system upon the unity of all beings.[1] Shumayyil held this maxim because he believed in the idea of progress and science. Following Spencer, Shumayyil wrote not only on the importance of scientific method, like most positivists, but also on the natural-philosophical system as a whole derived from the fundamental laws of physics and biological science. Although Spencer was unequivocally opposed to state regulation of public education and other social control, Shumayyil accepted such regulations because he believed that the duty of higher authority should encompass not only the protection of the rights of the individuals but also the harmonization of a society's social life.

Shumayyil, by all accounts, was the first Arab thinker among both Muslims and Christians to introduce coherent materialist ideas. Although he was not a creative philosopher like Darwin or Newton (some Arabs considered him to be the Bacon of the Arab world), he had a thorough grasp of the issues and an ability to give them lucid exposition. His statements were uncompromising, Shumayyil confessed to his readers. 'My problem, if it can be called a problem, is that when a certain truth appears to me, I cannot suppress it.'[2] In his view, science had to be studied because of its intrinsic, magnetic appeal.

The earliest Arab responses to Darwinism during the late nineteenth century took place at just about the same time that the battle over similar issues was raised by European, and especially by English Victorian writers.[3] In fact, the real debate began in Europe after the publication of the *Descent of Man* in 1871. The most significant controversies over Darwinism took place after the diffusion of Shumayyil's ideas on materialism during the early 1880s. It is safe to suggest that if Shumayyil had limited his translations to Büchner's commentaries on Darwin's ideas about speciation, the controversies might have been avoided altogether.[4] But he attempted to prove a relationship between the doctrine of evolution and materialistic thought, on one hand, and the origin of man, on the other hand. The attack on Shumayyil came from both religious and non-religious circles. It generated an enormous amount of publicity for Shumayyil's writings. This debate, and others like it, on subjects such as spontaneous generation, materialism and war, natural selection and animal intelligence helped to open new avenues in scientific thought among the Arab reading public.

Shumayyil understood Darwin's theory as a materialist creed. Influenced by other materialists, he upheld a universalist view based on a definite conception of the link between mind and matter, between thinking and being. He did not limit his discussion to the evolution of living things, but, following Spencer, he brought into focus the whole world of natural material components, inorganic and organic, and how these components interrelated in form and action.[5]

Shumayyil maintained that matter is the only reality. Form, energy and motion are the essence of the natural world. Matter never disappears and it is unchangeable, but it simply transforms from one condition or state to another.[6] When a body or anatomy seems to have faded away or a new figure seems to have originated, there is no creation or production of new matter, but rather only a permutation from one form to another. This attempt, by Shumayyil, to devise a dialectical law of the natural world resembles those laws which were formulated by Friedrich Engels.[7] Bezirgan indicates that Shumayyil never read Engels's work, but one is inclined to question his conclusion. Although Shumayyil was a medical doctor by training and his main interest was in Social Darwinism, there is evidence to suggest that his understanding of the physical sciences was formidable. He published a series of articles on electricity in *al-Jinan* (Gardens) before his graduation from SPC in 1871.[8] There he traced the history of electricity and physics from the ancient Greek era up to his time. He mentioned most well-known scientists and their inventions and experiments in this field. It is at least not impossible that Shumayyil had studied Engels's dialectical materialism while a student.

For Shumayyil, man is also a natural product of the world and all his physical components are derived naturally, exactly as with the rest of the animal kingdom. In his view, man has a direct relationship with the world of sense and comprehension. Nothing in man's material and physical structure, he maintained, could provide empirical verification of man's relationship with the spiritual world (*al-Arwah*) and metaphysics (*al-Ghayb*). In fact, Shumayyil emphasized that all elements going to constitute a human being are already existent in nature. From the physiological point of view, man is like an animal. What made man sentient was merely a quantitative summing up, rather than a qualitative leap.[9]

In his quest for scientism, Shumayyil advocated that natural sciences (*al-Ulum al-Tabiayah*) constitute the basis not only of human sciences (*al-Ulum al-Basharayah*) but of all sciences. He attributed the progress of Europe and the United States to their adoption of natural sciences, like physics, chemistry and geology; the backwardness of the East was due to its lack of interest in these sciences, which was replaced by an emphasis on theoretical and philosophical studies.[10] He advocated, in 1908, the abolition of law schools and university programmes in all other humanistic fields, like theology and linguistics, simply because they seemed useless to him.[11] In place of law, he proposed a school for chemistry, physics, mechanics, mathematics and astronomy. He wanted to substitute for the existing university structure a new one that emphasized natural history, natural sociology and natural economics (all of which could be applied to human beings), as well as medical, biological and other anthropological subjects. He suggested opening schools in every city and town according to the density of population. Children would be taught the principles of natural sciences and would come to comprehend the characteristics of water, air, inorganic matter, plants and animals. This natural education would help them understand the truth about man and his place in this world. He even advocated a social and medical programme for the whole population. He wanted to establish periodicals for instructing people how to be clean in dress, daily life and spirit. These publications would also teach that every natural system is subject to irrevocable natural laws. By following these rules people could avoid problems with their health, and in their material and moral lives. According to Shumayyil, the study of natural sciences would enhance human language and liberate man from the shackles of superstition.[12]

Shumayyil's ideas on materialism, brought him into direct confrontation with Muslim as well as with Christian writers. As we will see later, he debated materialism with Sarruf, and he sustained fierce attacks from Muslims and Christians on both scientific and religious grounds. To understand the Arab reaction to Western sciences, particularly their polemical orientation, a brief survey of the responses of Arab men and women of letters to Shumayyil's attack on their work is helpful.

While Shumayyil was preaching complete adoption of natural sciences after abolishing all literary education, he did not separate man from the world of literature. He wrote much poetry. Many men and women of letters debated the issue of literature with Shumayyil, the most prominent being Mayy Ziada, a woman distinguished in the field of classical Arabic literature. In an issue of *Majallat Sarkis*, a humourous periodical, Ziada wrote a lengthy letter to Shumayyil.[13] She explained that every human being, no matter how materialistic he was, had to be a poet some time.[14] She added that since the recent advance of natural sciences, a group of materialists advocated the inferiority of poetry and undermined not only literary knowledge but also everything that could not be sensed directly.[15] She went on to emphasize that, whereas in his view, man was created from matter and there was nothing in him except chemical components and red cells, in her view such materialism signified a life without hope. The sciences were incomplete without literature and the arts. She maintained that materialists harmed themselves by their attack on poets. They dreamed like poets. But materialists clothed their dreams in stone and metal, while poets made use of delicate and transparent silk. Ziada urged Shumayyil to limit his work to science and to avoid using violent language when describing poets and men of letters. She quoted Shumayyil's poetry to support her views. According to Ziada, the law of gravity in the cosmos was the same as the principle of love.[16] Shumayyil, in his reply to Ziada, praised her sensitivity, courage, and skill; he declared that he was not an enemy of literature and assured her that literature was the best part of science.[17]

Another reaction to Shumayyil's contempt for the theoretical sciences[18] came from Yusuf Shalhat, in a letter entitled 'Tanazu al-Baqa Bayn al-Ulum' (Struggle for Survival among the Sciences).[19] In response to *al-Muqtataf's* publication of Shumayyil's second introduction to Büchner's book on Darwin in 1909, Shalhat wrote that Shumayyil's introduction could serve only to destroy religion and law. He expressed his dismay at Shumayyil's attitude regarding the burning of the old Alexandria Library. Shumayyil had argued that the library was not a science library and therefore impeded man's search for truth. He stated that if Shumayyil's prophecy about the necessary disappearance of literary books in favour of books on natural sciences were true, then the former would become a 'missing link,' and future generations would search for this gap in knowledge much as scientists were then searching for the missing link in the chain of human evolution. Shalhat, like Mayy Ziada, criticized Shumayyil's harsh words directed against literary writers and drew his attention to the fact that scientists' new ideas can be assessed only by empirical evidence and not by personal attacks. He ended with a reminder to Shumayyil that man understands sciences by his mind, and philosophy is the science of mind. Therefore, philosophy is the mother of all sciences.[20]

Another letter to the editor of *al-Hilal*, entitled 'Ayy Ashadd Tathir fi Tarqiyyat shuun al-Ummah, al-Ulum al-Tabiiya am al-ulum al-Adabiya' (Which has More Impact on the Progress of a Nation, the Natural Sciences or the Literary Sciences?) came from Iskandar Damanhuri.[21] While he was responding to a query by *al-Hilal* on the same topic, it seems that Damanhuri was inspired by Shumayyil's original ideas on the natural sciences before the second introduction appeared in *al-Muqtataf*. Dumanhuri repeated Shummayil's arguments in favour of the natural sciences. Unlike Shumayyil, however, Damanhuri did not dismiss the value and the impact of literary sciences on natural knowledge. The progress of Europe and the advancement of society resulted, in his view, from the study of nature. He maintained that the work of natural scientists contributed to a wide variety of activities, including agriculture, commerce and manufacturing.[22] Professionals in these areas could hardly be held to have committed social crimes.[23] Damanhuri briefly digressed on what he called the 'biological axiom.' Just as the brain has a strong link with the stomach's digestive function, and just as circulation of the blood keeps the human mind active and healthy, so research in the literary sciences cannot provide human beings with new discoveries in nature. One could not, however, convince writers that their work was in vain:

> If one found a drunk man in the street and advised him to stop drinking, he would resort to mockery, no matter how eloquent and convincing was the argument that he heard; if one allowed the drinker to become sober after cleaning his stomach, he would feel sorry and strengthen his morals by himself.[24]

While many historians and scholars who have studied Shumayyil's work have correctly emphasized his rigorous materialistic and atheistic views, none has considered the possibility of an implicit theism in his work. Yet Sarruf wrote that when one read Shumayyil's writings one might think that Shumayyil was an ardent materialist; in fact, he was quite spiritual and superstitious.[25] Shumayyil himself noted in his writings: 'Oh God, give me patience, as I thank Him, even though people have accused me of being an atheist.'[26] Shumayyil's theism was even defended by a prominent Muslim scholar, Rashid Rida. In his response to Abd al-Kadir Qabani, another Muslim who had attacked Shumayyil's irreligious and Darwinian views, Rida asserted that Shumayyil's writing aimed, by scientific investigation, to provide evidence and support for religious rules. For Rida, Shumayyil did not seek to discredit religion, as such.[27]

Although his contemporaries considered him to be either an earnest materialist or a spiritualist, the fact remains that he was wholly unemotional in his search for the plain truth. He was a dedicated Arab thinker who was attracted to materialism and Darwinism as a kind of revenge for Arab attitudes towards modern sciences. Traditional Arab thinkers either could not comprehend Western natural sciences or perceived them as being hostile to religion. Arab intellectuals, especially those with an excellent command of classical Arabic literature, such as Nasif al-Yaziji and Ahmad Faris al-Shidyaq, were not interested in going beyond Arabic literary studies. Shumayyil was driven to his strong stand by the hostility of the Ottoman rulers towards the diffusion of progressive ideas among Arabs. These attitudes prevailed when the young Shumayyil was starting his writing career.

Shumayyil's attack on Arab traditional thought, as his writing revealed, did not prevent him from being the centre of Syrian social gatherings in Cairo. Descriptions of these gatherings appeared in the *Majallat Sarkis*. They featured witty criticism and light conversation about Shumayyil's ideas. Once Shumayyil suggested building a hospital for the poor. Responding to that suggestion, Sarkis, the editor of a journal, indicated that the concept of the survival of the fittest could be tested by experimental and observational methods. If the project of the hospital came at the right time, it would survive.[28] Sarkis also reported that Shumayyil was fond of playing 'Tawla' and 'Nard', popular games in the Arab world. Shumayyil liked to win at these games, and he sometimes forgot about his guests and food. Sarkis emphasized that if Shumayyil extended an invitation for lunch, one had to be sure that the 'Tawla did not compete with the food.'[29]

Darwinist thought

While Shumayyil recalled that he had first heard of Darwin's theory
in 1871, Sarruf's recollection was that Shumayyil first mentioned
Darwin's doctrine in 1870 while both were studying at the SPC.[30]
Both were dismayed to hear that the ape was man's ancestor.[31] The
two felt that this doctrine advocated the unity of creation and the
rejection of religious teaching on special creation. Shumayyil thought
that the system of education at the SPC did not help him to explore
Darwin's ideas. He studied Darwin without professional encourage-
ment. He tells us:

> In my graduation speech, surprisingly, I mentioned many facts that
> supported the doctrine [Darwin's theory] without realizing it. I did
> not realize that it would become the center of my thoughts and
> writing after graduation and travels in Europe.[32]

Shumayyil thought so highly of the theory of evolution that he wished
everyone to become familiar with its basic principles. Not to do so
indicated lack of courage. He considered Darwin's creed as the filter
through which controversial and competing human ideas might be
clarified. He felt that his new ideas would not really disturb the
tranquillity of Arab traditional thought, but rather would act like
yeast in dough.[33]

Shumayyil spent almost all of his philosophical energy on ex-
pounding Darwinism. Among the most remarkable of his accomplishments was his translation of Büchner's book on Darwin, which
he introduced with a long review of the social and philosophical
importance of Darwinism.[34] Shumayyil's introduction is a collection
of six essays in two segments: biological sciences and philosophy. The
translation, which contains the germs of materialism, created an
intellectual crisis among Arab thinkers. At this point it need only be
indicated that Shumayyil, as a result of attacks on his work, wrote
another book, *al-Haqiqa* (The Truth), in 1885 as an answer to his
critics.[35] In the latter book he dealt with the origin of life by arguing
in favor of spontaneous generation and against the germ theory.

He was nothing if not flexible. For this reason, the most striking
feature of Shumayyil's thought lies, not in the explosion of his
materialistic bomb, but in the echoes of this explosion which lasted
until the mid-1930s. A convenient way to follow the debates is by
examining the various issues involved: materialism, spontaneous
generation of life, the meaning of natural selection and the con-

troversy over religion and science. Darwin's theory did have an impact on religion, but it is unfair to describe Arab participants in the debate over evolution in terms of heroes who supported the theory and villains who opposed it. These issues will occupy us for the remainder of the present chapter.

Shumayyil's views on religion and evolution

Following the materialists, Shumayyil distinguished between knowledge and faith. He explained his experience with religion in terms of having passed from being a believer to a doubter and later to a non-believer. He started by asking himself:

> What is the cause of all causes and where is it? It is no doubt a force, but can force be identified without matter? No doubt it is exterior to matter. But how does it react with matter and at the same time remain separate from it? And if it is not separate from the force, how does it create others?[36]

Shumayyil was overwhelmed by this line of thought, which found expression in poems that he composed. Later Shumayyil considered the position of God in science, and he found no place for Him there. In his view, religion was the source of all social evils.[37] Yet, he attributed the cause of these social evils, not to religion itself, but to the men of religion. According to Shumayyil, religion is a human heritage and should be respected, while men of religion used religion for their own interests. As a Catholic, Shumayyil did not differentiate among religions. He based his arguments on the united nature of the universe. Rejecting the argument for the existence of God which was offered by revelation, he maintained a form of agnosticism.

Shumayyil made it clear that he valued an international interest in humanity which transcended national boundaries. This was to be the religion of mankind (Din al-Bashariyah). He attributed the introduction of torture and the burning of those who had diseases like epilepsy and mental disorders to the rise of spiritualists.[38] Shumayyil underlined that the origin of all religious dogmas were in essence due to the fear of the unknown and he applied Darwin's theory of natural selection to religion. Just as species evolved from one origin and the fittest could survive the external environment, the success of religions depended on their accommodation to prevailing conditions.[39]

Shumayyil's enthusiasm for the future victory of natural science and his interest in humanity as a whole seems out of place in our time. He did not live to witness the recent anti-science movement in the West and the anti-technology movement in the East, as manifested in the Iranian Revolution. As we will see later, Shumayyil also failed to foresee that the arguments for the survival of the fittest may be stretched to justify inter-racial struggles.

SALAMA MUSA

Scientific thought

By all accounts Musa was a disciple of Shumayyil. He was an ardent supporter of Darwin's theory throughout his life. Like Shumayyil, he was controversial. His revolutionary views continued to spread throughout the Arab world, especially between 1919 and 1939, and were the subject of many interpretations.

It seems that Musa led an isolated life because of his peculiar views on Egyptian society. His views brought him into confrontation with authority: his journals were closed or confiscated, and he served a jail sentence. Like Shumayyil, he viewed science not only as a line of thought but as a unique approach and the best method of studying the order of things. In his quest for the scientific spirit, Musa stayed very close to the path marked by the scientific accomplishments of the West in the nineteenth century. His concerns coincided with those of other Arab secularists, like Shumayyil, who believed that science was transforming their society. Unlike Shumayyil, he was not trained in science. He was a journalist who had become acquainted with scientific ideas.

In his book *Haula Allamuni* (Those Who Taught Me), Musa acknowledged the influence of more than twenty European thinkers and philosophers, including Chaim Weissmann, Darwin, Albert Schweizer, Goethe, John Dewey, Thoreau, Hendrik Ibsen, H. G. Wells, Nietzsche, Doestoevsky, Marx and G. B. Shaw.[40] Among Arab thinkers who also influenced Musa's thought were Lutfi al-Sayyid, Shumayyil, Sarruf, Farah Antun and Jurji Zaydan.[41] While Musa's political and social activity is not our main concern here, it is noteworthy that he was the first to call for the creation of an Egyptian socialist party in 1921.

Musa was a co-founder of a society to transmit modern science and its application to the Arab world, and his model was the British Association for the Advancement of Science. It was called the Egyptian Society for Scientific Culture (al-Majma al-Misri Lil al-Thaqafa al-Ilmiyyah). In addition to Musa, Sarruf's nephew, other professors of science at Cairo University and some directors of the Egyptian government were founders of the society. It took shape in 1929 and its first publication appeared in 1930.[42] Later, the society expelled Musa for his political writings.

Like Shumayyil, Musa was both persistent and outspoken after his own fashion without fear of contradicting prevailing thought. He sought to liberate women from an unfree status that was contrary to the law of evolution. He advocated giving women equal opportunities in life, just as their counterparts had obtained in Europe. In this respect, Musa did not follow Shumayyil, who insisted on the natural inferiority of women because they had smaller brains than men.

Musa asserted that science was the primary feature of Western culture and had a great impact on literature and morals.[43] While Musa recognized the fact that the West had fought an uphill battle with traditional thought in order to establish the scientific spirit, democracy, and women's liberation, the Arab East still resisted such change.[44] Under the influence of Marxist ideology, Musa emphasized that the rise and development of a culture followed prevailing economic conditions. The mode of production and the method of distribution of wealth determined the cultural system of a country. European culture and scientific ideas were the end products of the industrial revolution, exactly as backward traditions and corruption in Eastern culture were outcomes of an agricultural society.[45] Musa urged the Arab East to adopt Western science and embark on industrialization; only after this development was accomplished could the value system change. He emphasized that the more he came to know the East, the more he hated it and felt a stranger in his own land. The more he learned about Europe, the more he became attached to it.[46] This sentiment reminds us of what Khedive Ismail, ruler of Egypt from 1863 to 1879, said sixty years previously 'Mon pays ce n'est pas en Afrique, mais en Europe.' Arab culture, Musa maintained, should be understood in order to be avoided, for its negative features include slavery, despotism and dependence on gods. Musa advocated the replacement of the Arabic alphabet by the Latin one.

Musa affirmed his belief in the superiority of the scientific culture of modern civilization over the literary one. The latter, which dominated the Arab mind, consisted of Arabic literature and language. It represented the non-scientific mind of primitive society. Therefore, according to Musa, societies that lived in a past which condoned slavery and despotism could not produce scientific culture. Science flourished with the abolition of slavery and when the people were given access to education and wealth. To elaborate this point, Musa cited French thinkers of the late eighteenth and early nineteenth centuries, who concentrated in their writing on the importance of science and described Newton as one of the greatest men of all time. Musa asserted that any savage could compose poetry, while science was the result modern civilization and sophisticated minds.[47] For Egypt to be admitted to the modern age of science and industry, it had to break completely with the corrupt past, assimilate Western scientific culture, and foster a scientific environment.[48]

The dedicated Darwinian

Musa's admiration of evolution is apparent throughout his work. He wrote that 'socialism and evolution were the seeds of my cultural growth, to which I could relate all my ideas on social, moral or religious analysis'.[49] He produced more than 40 books during his life, and in every one of them he mentioned evolutionary theory.[50] His major works on Darwin and evolution include two books and an essay on *Muqdimat al-Superman* (The Advent of Superman). The books are *Nazariyat al-Tatawwur wa-Asl al-Insan* (The Theory of Evolution and the Origin of Man) and *Al-Insan Qimmat al-Tatawwur* (Man is the Acme of Evolution). Musa contributed many articles on the same topic in the pages of the journals *al-Muqtataf*, and *al-Hilal* as well as in his own journal *al-Majalla al-Jadida* (The New Journal).[51] He was explicit about his debt to Darwin:

I do not know of any writer by whom I was more influenced than Darwin. He gave me the tools to destroy tradition. He made evolution the theme of my thought and my human ideology, which is far from metaphysics. I started to evaluate nations by their evolutionary process. Evolution in its essence is a scientific idea, but for me, it is also an emotional doctrine. Therefore, I must consider Darwin my first teacher.[52]

Musa was introduced to Darwin's theory and to Büchner's ideas on evolution by Shumayyil before leaving for Europe in 1908. Musa sojourned in France and England at an early stage of his intellectual development. He was in his early twenties when he came to know about the revolutionary ideas of nineteenth-century science and evolution. The seminal ideas about evolution planted by Shumayyil and Sarruf flowered during the year that Musa spent in London as a member of the social-democratic Fabian Society. These were the years when the critic and dramatist George Bernard Shaw participated with the Fabians and developed his ideas on the superman. From writings of men like Spencer, he may have come to know about the application of Darwin's biological ideas on evolution to social sciences and philosophy. From the Eugenics Society under the leadership of Francis Galton, a society to which Musa also belonged, he learned about the work of Nietzsche and Ludovic on the future masters of the world.

While still in London, Musa publicized his new knowledge in two articles for *al-Muqtataf* and one brief essay. The first article appeared in the issue of July 1909 and it is entitled 'Nietzsche wa-Ibn al-Insan' (Nietzsche and the Son of Man).[53] There Musa described Nietzsche's *Thus Spake Zarathustra*, Ludovic's *Who Is to Be the Master of the World* and Shaw's *Man and Superman*. Musa explained that his aim was not to describe the methods used by the British authorities to improve the breeding stock of their nation, but rather to draw the attention of Eastern readers to factors that contributed to weak racial stock, for example, allowing physically and mentally handicapped persons to marry and not encouraging those with physical and mental health to produce children. Accepting the schemes of the eugenicists to improve the world by selective breeding, he nevertheless emphasized that one had to free mother nature from human influence if one wanted to better future generations.[54] He asked, 'Why do we see a great resemblance between old Egyptian *mumiyat* (mummies) and present, Coptic humans?' His answer was that 'we stand against nature, and that is why Nietzsche spends his life explaining the mistakes that humans have committed by blocking the return to regular natural laws.'[55] Following Nietzsche and Shaw, Musa emphasized that the shepherd applied the law of natural selection by choosing the strongest male to mate with his ewes; if humans were reluctant to do so, then the fate of human society would be uncertain.[56] One was not to avoid providing help and mercy to the handicapped, but it would be a crime to permit such people to marry and produce another handicapped generation.

By 1930, Musa modified his views on the idea of the superman. In the first of two editorials in his journal *al-Majalla al-Jadida*, entitled 'Al-Tabiyah wa-al Insaniya'[57] (Nature and Humanity), he repeated the British biologist Arthur Keith's remarks on the justifications of war as the best method for the survival of the fittest among nations. He reiterated Nietzsche's views on this notion and declared that even though 'we are under the influence of the principle of nature and the human principle, man in his social life adhered to both principles'.[58] He suggested that the latter principle takes precedence over the former. Musa added that it is true that war contributed to the survival of strong nations, but at the same time war also caused the death of the very fittest. In his second editorial, entitled 'al-Taaqum wa al-Yujiniyyh' (Sterilization and Eugenics) Musa criticized Nietzsche's idea on the obliteration of the weak and labelled it as sophism and unpractical for the future human race. Yet, he praised Galton's work on genius and inheritance, which encouraged the sterilization of the handicapped and early marriage for the fit.[59]

Musa's second article appeared in the same journal in May 1910, and bore the title 'Nazariyyat al-Nushu al-Hadira' (Present Theories of Evolution).[60] Like Shumayyil, he showed a nuanced grasp of the theory of evolution. Musa briefly described Darwin's ideas on natural selection, Lamarck's and Spencer's on acquired characteristics, Samuel Butler's views opposing Lamarck and Spencer, Weissmann's argument on acquired characteristics and De Vries' ideas on mutation. He viewed selective breeding as the only means for human progress.[61] Sarruf, in his reply to Musa's article, favoured De Vries' views on mutation by saying that they were the best ideas advocated on the subject.[62]

Musa's third work from the London period was an essay on the meaning of superman, *Muqadimat al-Superman*, published in 1909. In it he discussed, among other things, the idea of future human evolution and the superman. He punctuated his book with quotations from European thinkers, repeating Shaw's idea on voluntary sterilization for the mentally and physically handicapped.

Shumayyil was unhappy with Musa's notions. According to Shumayyil, Shaw's advocacy of the notion of superman, as elaborated in Musa's *Muqadimat al-Superman*, was a 'corrupt concept' because Shaw based his conviction not on Darwin's doctrine of natural selection but on artificial or man-made selection (Al-Intikhab al-Sinaia). The latter sought to create a superman.[63] Shumayyil remarked that Shaw agreed with Schopenhauer and Nietzsche on killing the unfit and keeping the healthy. Shumayyil described Nietzsche, Shaw and Schopenhauer as dreamers with vivid imaginations. While Shumayyil basically agreed with their interpretation of Darwin's natural laws, he disagreed with the blind application of these laws to society.[64]

The notion of superman was further elaborated on by Wahba Musa, who was probably Salama Musa's son, in a three page commentary entitled 'Limadha Nahnu Duafa' (Why We are Weak) which appeared in *al-Majalla al-Jadida* in 1930.[65] Wahba Musa asked why so many scientists were occupied with the issue of human physical weakness instead of weakness in other animal species. In his view, mind was the cause of human weakness, because when a person lost his mind through mental illness he became physically stronger. He provided the example of the orangutang who started his life with a high degree of intelligence. Later, as the ape grew older, its mental power decreased as a result of its increase in physical strength. The author added that the same relationship existed also among plants, for trees that bear fruit are weaker and less beautiful than other trees. He provided further evidence to support the proposition that human physical weakness was the end result of the development of mind. Geniuses were most likely to have poor health because their high intellectual power drained a great deal of their physical strength. He used the example of Darwin's poor health and his inability to work more than three hours a day. Wahba concluded that man could not become a superman with a giant head in the future, because this would overtax the physical resources of the human body. Therefore, the author maintained, the notion of superman was only a theoretical concept and could not be attained in practice.[66] He concluded that an old saying, 'a healthy mind in a healthy body', should be changed to read 'a healthy mind in a sick body'.

Salama Musa's other major work on Darwinism is *Nazariyat al-Tatawwur wa Asl al-Insan* (Theory of Evolution and the Origin of Man), published in 1928. He wrote the book in order to fill a gap in the Arabic language on the study of evolution. Musa sought to explain the theory of evolution in simple language accessible to ordinary readers. The book is divided into two sections: the first develops the evolutionary concept before the appearance of man and the second discusses human evolution.

Following Shumayyil and Spencer, Musa wrote, 'Evolution is a comprehensive law that covers the world of organic and inorganic matter.'[67] He maintained that living organisms and innate matter are in constant development and change. Evolution, for Musa, was 'the theory of hope and progress and the key that can open our obscure past and indicate the fate of human kind.'[68] Musa, in his book, compiled basic information on evolutionary theory and did not depart greatly from his earlier views. The theory of evolution, Musa noted, contributed to almost every aspect of human knowledge. In this way, educators, politicians and philosophers, among others, were guided by the notion of progressive development to explain and understand certain elements of human nature. Musa asked whether a philosopher could explore the essence of human spirit without knowing the evolution of the human nervous system and its relationship with lower animals.[69]

In the chapter on the origin of life, 'Asl al-Hayat', Musa almost paraphrased Shumayyil's views on life and matter. He wrote that life was one form of matter, just as the mind was one form of life, and the elements that constituted the living organism could be found in inorganic matter.[70] How life came about in the first cell, Musa did not know. He also found no difference exists between plants and animals in terms of breeding, nutrition and growth, except in exterior shape.

With regard to the term 'struggle for survival', Musa seems to have provided an explanation that contradicted his convictions on the idea of superman. The latter term did not indicate a physical struggle between two opposing individuals. The struggle might also be between individuals and environmental factors such as temperature or lack of food. He added that co-operation among living organisms, could in many instances help the process of evolution.[71]

Confronted with a disturbing question on the origin of man, Musa indicated that Darwin and Huxley did not insist that man originated from the ape. They cautiously mentioned that the difference between the lower and the higher apes was greater than the one between the latter and man. Musa wrote that man and ape came from one species that was neither human nor simian. He quoted Cruikshank's argument that both man and ape had a common father, a standing man-ape, the remains of which had been discovered in Java. Musa added that Asian man resembled the Asian monkey in hand prints and in bearing; African and European man bore a distinct resemblance to the chimpanzee.[72]

Musa also remarked on the human brain. He wrote that it was not the size of the human brain and the number of its parts that makes men superior to other animals, but rather man's ability to communicate through language. Therefore, according to Musa, it was language that generated the large brain of man and not the reverse.[73]

Musa devoted many sections in his book to the emergence of human society and the impact of fire, food, language, marriage, magic, dress and religion on the struggle for survival.[74] Still influenced by the notion of superman, he wrote that the struggle for survival no longer really worked because, unlike the days when only the strong and the courageous could marry, marriage had come to take place regardless of individual weaknesses. This practice hindered the evolution of mankind. Therefore, Musa added, the creation of the Eugenics Society was necessary to substitute artificial selection for unworkable natural selection. Musa described a future man who would be different from present man, especially in the increased size of his brain, disappearance of toes, hair, stomach and lower colon, and increased visual acuity.[75]

The last chapter in the book concerned Darwin's biography and his work which, according to Musa, gave humanity a new vision of life far from the metaphysical world. He deplored the fact that the Egyptian Ministry of Education encouraged the teaching of old Arab literary subjects rather than Darwin's teachings. For this reason, among others, Musa reiterated that the Egyptian nation was still Oriental and had not evolved as far as it should have.[76]

Religion and evolution

Musa was preoccupied with the idea of God. Drawing on Shumayyil, Musa turned away from divine religion, preferring to have his own religion of science and human culture. He believed that religion, a human innovation, developed with the advancement of life.[77] Musa applied the theory of evolution to the development of religion as well as to other human activities. Islam, Christianity and Judaism reached the stage of monotheism only after a long history of struggle and progress.[78]

Musa echoed Nietzsche's outcry that God had died. By saying so, he thought that the Egyptian peasant (*fallah*) would be liberated from religious slavery.[79] Darwinism could serve as a weapon against the religious establishment, which hindered the natural process of evolution. Comparing religious studies with theose of the physical sciences, Musa argued that material and natural sciences were far in advance of other fields like religion, literature and politics.

A man could argue that iron is not an element, but a compound, and if anyone disagreed with him, the challenge could be conducted in a good manner and based on experimental ground. While if somebody else called for adopting Bolshevik ideas or claimed that marriage to two women is better than to one, he would find stiff resistance from some individuals and would find himself morally discredited or physically eliminated.[80]

Musa maintained that no progress could be achieved until complete freedom of thought was permitted in religious discussion exactly as in the case of the physical sciences.

It was unfortunate, he continued, to see scientists searching for the origin of matter and the secret of the universe, while traditionalists were still defending old religious and social dogmas and expected people to believe in them through the power of customary law.[81] According to Musa, Darwin's theory struck a blow against religion when it denied special creation. At the same time, this theory weakened the confidence in the human mind, largely because of its relativist side. Kant and Bergson had provided a new outlook on and respect for religion. Kant believed that man could not comprehend mere facts, but was only aware by his projection or perception of phenomena. In other words, Musa noted: 'We do not know the things we see in this world, but we know our thought or projection of them.'[82] Thus, according to Musa's peculiar reasoning, Kant's ideas actually supported materialism. He thought that Bergson's 'creative evolution' was much in the Kantian tradition.[83]

Musa's most interesting views on the subject came in his discussion of the triangular relationship between religion, literature and science. According to him, literature strives for beauty and tranquility, while the aim of science is planning and assessment. Science explains certain measurements, quantities and phenomena. Literature tackles spirit, beauty, hopes, people, their agony and despair. Therefore, Musa noted, religion is literature; it focuses on human morals, unlike science which focuses on experimentation. Any man of letters (*Adib*) who deals with morals and ethics has the right to be judged from the religious point of view.[84] Religion, for Musa, is simply a set of moral and ethical rules. For this reason he managed to identify philosophers with theologians, prophets and other human reformers. They aimed to help human progress and eliminate tyranny and exploitation.

Conclusion

What can be learned from Musa's version of Darwinism? To be sure, his work has been taken seriously by many Arab scholars. He debated issues with other Arab thinkers on controversial topics; his critics were more numerous than his admirers.[85] Musa devoted more than fifty years to propagating his views and wrote more than forty books. He found himself in an age increasingly directed by science and for this reason, perhaps, he was bitter about the stagnation of the Arab world. He looked askance at scholars who directed their efforts to revive the old Arab literary movement. He was disappointed to see Arab intellectual energy wasted on the study of literature, while Westerners devoted their time to science. Musa's secular views and his attack on traditional Arab morality constituted a new departure in Arab social reform.

Musa held a deep conviction that total Westernization of Egypt was essential. His call for the adoption of Darwin's theory, though, did not entitle him to call himself the scientific, objective scholar that he imagined himself to be. Musa was overwhelmed by Western science. Adopting extreme views in his writing provided an outlet for his growing dissatisfaction with the metaphysical failures of Arab society. He intended to demonstrate, by exaggeration, the value gap between the world of science and the world of literature.

Musa's work combines two opposing ideologies: the call for Nietzsche's idea of superman on the one hand, and the advancement of socialism by the ideals of the Fabian Society on the other. While Musa's antagonism to imperialism was loud and clear, he was fond of quoting H. G. Wells's colonialist motto, 'The world is our village'.[86] As another example of his fragmented personality, Musa combined Nietzsche's thought on the elimination of the weak with Marx's views on the scientific interpretation of history and the revolution against capitalism.

As a writer about science Musa did not have the disinterested vision of a scientist. He was probably never truly concerned with science as an end in itself, but rather as a means to industrial development that could bring Egypt up to his vision of the European standard. We have seen Musa's skepticism about the inability of traditional Arab institutions to come to grips with European science and how he was greatly excited to have found in Darwin's theory a way of achieving progress in the East. Musa's absolute belief and his assertion of the extreme truth of Darwin's views could classify him as a dogmatic writer, but such a judgement must not obscure his dedication and sincere commitment to liberate the Arab masses from tyranny and exploitation.

YAQUB SARRUF

By all accounts, Sarruf was a pioneer who introduced modern scientific thought to the Arab world. He launched the most influential scientific journal in the Arab East of the time, *al-Muqtataf*. Like Shumayyil a native of Lebanon and graduate of the SPC, Sarruf was one year older than Shumayyil. Unlike Shumayyil and Musa, he was very careful and moderate in his writing and this enhanced his influence. In *al-Muqtataf*, Sarruf was adamant in his argument to distinguish between established scientific ideas and mere speculation, no matter how widespread popular acceptance might be.

Sarruf recalled how he and Shumayyil first learned about Darwin's theory and how he then thought of its impact on religious values. Sarruf discussed Darwin's theory and Darwinism with conviction and deep understanding. But at the time and in the milieu in which he found himself, Sarruf avoided direct confrontation with religious institutions. As editor of *al-Muqtataf*, Sarruf received scores of letters from Arab thinkers of the time who erroneously credited the theory of evolution to Arab philosophers. While Sarruf refused to engage in polemical debate, he managed to answer their letters in a highly convincing fashion.

While Sarruf was a convert to Darwin's creed, unlike Shumayyil, he categorically denounced materialism and can be considered a religious Darwinist. He urged readers to adopt the natural sciences and Darwin's theory, which was not in contradiction with the word of God. He maintained that the Holy Books were not intended to teach science. He defended Darwin against his critics – especially as shown in the case of Edwin Lewis, an American professor at the SPC in 1882.

Sarruf's interest ranged over many subjects; he was conversant in mathematics, philosophy and literature. He was also one of the key scholars who introduced many new scientific, biological and literary terms that have since been incorporated into the body of the Arabic language. The terms *Tatawwur* (evolution), *Darwiniyya* (Darwinism) and *Tanazu al-baqa* (struggle for life) spring readily to mind.[87]

Sarruf not only added new terms to enrich Arabic, but he revived forgotten and archaic ones as well, and he introduced the Western scientific style of writing in Arabic. Traditional writing was characterized by long introductions and long conclusions in which writers contributed apologies to the effect that they were not *bona fide* experts and asked almighty God to help in the endeavour. Writers would end their texts with the term *Allah aalam* (God is more knowledgeable.) Sarruf attacked his subject in a direct fashion without using such stylistics. This new form of writing was imitated by many educated Arabs.

Sarruf always refused to believe or mention any scientific assumption without conclusive evidence. He was perhaps the least dogmatic of Arab scientific scholars as he borrowed from many disciplines in an eclectic fashion. Like Shumayyil and Musa, Sarruf emphasized the role of natural and mathematical sciences, for these were essential to the search for truth. But unlike Shumayyil, Sarruf made it mandatory for students to study natural and mathematical sciences as well as social and historical disciplines.[88] In his view, by studying social, historical and natural topics, students could find material to write about; by studying arithmetic, algebra, geometry and logic, students could distinguish between good and bad judgements.[89]

He had a tendency to make practical use of scientific principles. When he was studying at the SPC he built a mechanical mill.[90] He was the first to teach toxicology (*Ilm al-Sumum*) in Arabic, and, according to Shumayyil, in 1871 he became the first to write in Arabic on Pasteur's concept of germs. [91] Shumayyil also added that Sarruf was the first to introduce to Arabic readers certain Darwinist thoughts and at the same time to refute them as if he were a creationist himself.[92]

Sarruf covered a wide spectrum of subjects. He taught Arabic literature, natural philosophy and mathematics at the SPC. He reserved a section in *al-Muqtataf* for debate on sophisticated mathematical questions in arithmetic, algebra, geometry, trigonometry, logarithms, calculus and astronomy. He also published a book on astronomy, *Bassait Ilm al-Falak* (Introduction to Astronomy) in 1923, in addition to scores of articles written or translated on different aspects of astronomy and mathematics. In physics, chemistry, biology, history and philosophy, Sarruf introduced in his journal the most prominent scientists of the field, including Darwin, Spencer, Bergson and Büchner. While we are concerned with Sarruf's views on Darwinism, it is important to indicate his reaction to certain controversies regarding the impact of Darwinian ideas on other branches of knowledge. This impact revolved around the following issues: materialism, the meaning of natural selection and the survival of the fittest, animal intelligence, science and religion, and the spontaneous generation of life. In the next chapter I consider these points in turn.

4 Secularist Christian Responses to Controversies About Darwinism

THE DEBATE OVER MATERIALISM

The introduction of materialism to the Arab East by Shumayyil was a shock to the whole Islamic world. One of the earliest reactions came from Faris Nimr in a long address delivered to an Arab charitable society called 'Shams al-Birr.' It was entitled 'Fasad Falsafat al-Madiyyin' (The Corruption of Materialistic Philosophy), and appeared in *al-Muqtataf* in 1883.[1] The writer set out to expose the principal error of materialistic ideology, which advocated that the actions of the soul are the same as the actions of matter. For materialists, feelings, emotions, intellect and human will were simply actions of the brain.[2]

Nimr was unhappy to see Beirut youth adopting what he called empty principles, like materialism, without verifying the truth of its assumptions. While Nimr did not disapprove of many of the scientific explanations of nature provided by the materialists, he felt that this philosophy could be refuted on scientific grounds, in fact, on the same grounds that the materialists provided to support their own claims.[3] Nimr asserted that the materialists had two strong arguments in support of their views: the relation between brain and mind, on the one hand, and the physical law of conservation of energy, on the other. As to the first point, he rejected the ideas that matter or brain was the cause of intellect and that the mind was the action of the brain. Instead, Nimr held that the mutual interaction between brain and mind is strong, and when the brain of an animal increased in size, the animal's strength also increased. When the brain got

51

weaker by means of disease or age the mind also got weaker in its action:

> Our knowledge of the existence of matter or substance is condi-
> tional on our mental judgement, and without mind itself, we might
> not be able to trace matter.[4]

Here Nimr cited an address of John Tyndall to the British Association for the Advancement of Science. In it Tyndall admitted that the
transformation of the brain's action to conscious and mental action is
beyond reason. Nimr also denied that the law of the equilibrium of
forces supported the claim of materialism. He held that, on the
contrary, it rejected them. If this law applied to brain and mind, he
wrote, then the human mind should be a force similar to other
natural forces, a sort of motion, as in the case of light, temperature
and electricity. Nimr added that this was impossible, even if scientists
found a scale to measure intellect just as they measure temperature,
or a scale to measure love just as they measure electricity. Materialists still could not substantiate their claim because the human mind is
not like any other natural forces and has no motion.[5] Here Nimr
upheld the traditional distinction between matter and spirit.

MATERIALISM AND WAR

The debate over materialism and its impact on war stemmed from a
speech entitled 'Life and Matter in War' which was delivered on 13
December 1914 by Henri Bergson, before the annual meeting of the
French Academy of Literary and Political Science, of which he was
president. A summary of the address was translated by *al-Muqtataf*
and appeared in its April 1916 issue.[6] Bergson examined the industrial configuration of Germany, which had been the dominant feature
of Prussia's policy of integrating other German states purely on a
basis of what they could provide for industrial development. He
condemned the military build-up of Germany before and after the
1870 war with France, as well as the uses of natural sciences for
purely materialistic gains.[7] He bitterly attacked the misuse by the
Germans of their technology. Bergson viewed such transgressions as
clear examples in favour of war, because there was no moral deter-
rent to prevent Germany's atrocities.[8] People saw this materialistic
success as a way to justify any immoral principle. 'Force and right are
alike', he asserted. When the force decided to follow a new path, all

rights disappeared. He also abhorred the way German philosophers and poets provided blind support for such materialistic gains. When Germany became expansionist, it justified its policy by Hegel's principles, just as it provided evidence of its admiration for literary beauty by drawing on Kant and for passion by drawing on Schopenhauer. And if Germany decided to justify another action for which no support could be found among her own thinkers, it drew on ideas that had been derived from foreign philosophers. The complexity of the disagreements between the moralists and the materialists leads one to appreciate Bergson's conclusions. Bergson added that no matter how Germany attempted to subjugate moral forces to material gain, the moral forces would rise up and prove that they were the masters of material forces.

Commenting on Bergson's attack on German materialistic policy, Dr Amin Abu Khatir refuted the putative German philosophy of war, which was based on the principles of natural selection and survival of the fittest.[9] There was a parallel to the German scientists' interpretation of biological laws to justify war and inter-racial struggle. Khatir suggested the German philosophers claimed that:

War is a struggle for survival and it is the end product of natural selection. Because the German nation is strong, it must struggle with weak nations so that the weak will perish and the strong survive.[10]

Contrary to what the German said, Khatir stressed that the laws of selection deal precisely with the survival of the fittest and not the existence of the strongest. He rejected the German idea that physical strength alone is the only requirement to survive in life. He added:

If we put a lion in a cage, it will die from hunger, but if we imprisoned a man, he could survive, because he continually thinks about how to preserve his life.[11]

He went on to say that, if we put both man and lion in the cage, the lion will kill the man even though it is less fit than he. He dismissed the German philosophy of war as contrary to all biological laws. Life on earth had never been a struggle between individuals in the sense that some killed and others survived, for if this were so, one could not explain the extinction of huge and very strong animals. Progress in controlling nature and its forces for man's needs had replaced blind, natural selection. In this light, he showed his admiration for man-made selection by praising the effort of modern civilization in controlling diseases, and thus in reducing the death rate among children and helping the handicapped.

Abu Khatir rejected the notion that strength is a pillar to natural selection. If Pasteur and Johnson (a boxing champion of that time) engaged in a boxing match, no doubt Pasteur would lose even though he was more fit than the former to survive, because Pasteur served science and humanity. He concluded that, in addition to military strength, one also needed morality, ethics and reason to win a war.[12] He gave direct support to Bergson's portrayal of the barbaric German war. Germans, Khatir noted, had confused biology and moral principles and misinterpreted the scientific meaning of biological principles with social understanding.

SARRUF AND SHUMAYYIL ON MATERIALISM

In the March 1916 issue of *al-Muqtataf*, Sarruf cited an excerpt on materialism and spiritualism from Shumayyil's philosophical poems, 'al-Rojhan'.[13] In it Shumayyil repeated his traditional attack on spiritual concepts, religion and all that was not materialistic.[14] Commenting on Shumayyil's poem, Sarruf mentioned that Shumayyil probably composed it before the start of World War I, the end product of materialistic philosophy. Sarruf underlined the significance of the divine force in creating the material world, as well as in organizing and controlling every aspect of it. Sarruf also emphasized that there were certain events in this material world that did not run according to existing rules and regulations.

> Why is there such excess production of fish eggs and tree fruits, so many animals that kill each other, diseases that attack the undeserving and bad rulers commanding good people?[15]

Again Sarruf showed that there was wisdom behind events that could not be understood. He criticised Shumayyil's urging of people to accept what they know as absolute facts. Sarruf concluded:

> Our opinions about the universe do not have to be associated with the right judgement, but rather they depend on our health, whether we are sick or tired; and on the stomach, whether it is strong or weak.[16]

Unhappy about Sarruf's remarks on materialism and war, Shumay-yil wrote a short article entitled 'al-Falsafah al-Madiyyah, Haqiqa-tuha wa Nataijuha' (Materialist Philosophy: Its Truth and Its Results).[17] In it he posed more questions than he answered. He asked whether the war was a result of this doctrine. If science contributed to the destructive capability of war, he questioned whether past wars were less destructive, comparatively, than the ongoing war. 'What is materialist philosophy and its teaching in human sociology?' Shumay-yil asked. Materialist philosophy is just another name for the philos-ophy of self-interest, he answered, and it is this philosophy that is the cause of this war. Was 'the philosophy of self-interest' an 'evil of education'? Shumayyil answered this latter question by posing another one. 'Were past wars waged for self-interest? Is it not self-interest that stimulates all our actions whether good or bad, material or moral, earthly or unearthly? Who does not pursue his interests?'[18] Shumay-yil not only suggested that self-interest could stimulate human actions, but also that a misconception of it led most people to act so that their interests conflicted with those of others. This circumstance is the cause of social regression. More importantly, Shumayyil maintained that 'materialist doctrine was *alm al-Tabiah* [natural science]'. He then asked how nature related to human interests. In his view, the public interest (al-Maslaha al-Amma) is 'natural' in all its actions, but the public interest depends on the private interest; if this were not so, a unified system could not be produced from separate units and individ-uals could not be organized in a social order.[19] In this way, nature is also concerned with the common interest. He also emphasized the cruelty of nature, pointing out that nature is wasteful. This harshness, according to him, is essential to ensure that life continues.[20]

Shumayyil doubted that war could ever be justified by materialistic philosophy – even if the distinguished scientists taught that that was the case. Nevertheless, he added, while there is always struggle among all units of a living body and as a result many victims may fall, still this struggle is a co-operative one and necessary for the survival of the body itself.[21] This action for survival serves the public interest at large. Shumayyil believed that only a misunderstanding of materi-alism and of possible benefit to individuals could have led to the ongoing war.[22] Shumayyil concluded that the materialist philosophy was not responsible for the war, and that a deep understanding of the common interest could have prevented it. The causes of the war were greed and a lack of understanding of the basic concept of material-ism. Ignorance among advanced nations was more acute than had been thought. Here, Shumayyil does not seem to relinquish or compromise any of his materialistic views. It is not surprising, therefore, that he insisted that distortion of the materialistic philosophy of interest, public or common, yielded the principles of war.[23]

Sarruf, in a rejoinder to Shumayyil, quoted a line from Shumayyil's poem where Shumayyil compared the enlightened age to the oppressive and tyrannical one when religion was the dominant force.[24] This line recalled to Sarruf the atrocities committed by the Germans in the war. The author advised Shumayyil to read Bergson's speech and Abu Khatir's exposition of it. Sarruf found that the materialists' philosophy taught people to believe only in matter and its laws without regard to anything else. He continued that this philosophy had most in common with Spencer (who said that the Creator was unknown and unknowable), and then went further to an uncompromising materialism, even denying God could exist independently from matter. If this philosophy were right and the German atrocities could be justified by it, Sarruf wrote:

> What would prevent a man from killing anybody who hinders his progress exactly as he kills lions, wolves and flies? Why should not a man from Paris or Berlin then kill Blacks who prevent him from hunting in a forest in Africa? Is not the deterrent that keeps strong people from having a free hand with weak people, a moral one rather than a materialistic one?[25]

He provided a distinction between animals (Ajamawat) which have lived harmoniously for millions of years without killing each other, like ants and bees, and lived only under the prevailing natural laws, and humans, who deviated from this rule and provided a new ethos, according to which, when one group of people found themselves more advanced than another, it would dominate them. The next step was for this ethos to be substantiated on scientific grounds, as the German philosophers did. Sarruf held that the Germans and not the English behaved with their colonies in this brutal manner, because the English still held allegiance to their religion, which teaches that men are brothers.

Sarruf denied that materialism could prevent wars and direct people to live in harmony. In his view, materialism was responsible for war. People in other areas of the world were ignorant of materialist principles, yet crimes there were not commonplace. He cited certain telegrams received by *al-Muqatam*, which gave witness to the atrocities committed by the Germans who supported materialism, in contrast to the human and merciful actions conducted by the English, French, Russian, Turkish and Arab officers in the war.[26]

THE MEANING OF NATURAL SELECTION AND THE SURVIVAL OF THE FITTEST

Horrified by the war, Jurji Zaydan, the editor of *al-Hilal* delivered a speech on 'al-Insanyah al-Qadimah' (The Future of Mankind) at the YMCA in Cairo.[27] It appeared in his journal in 1915. He quoted European writers, without mentioning their names, on how humans would cope in the future with the consequences of the struggle for survival. He attributed the increase of mental disease, and the increase of alcoholism and suicide, as consequences of this struggle. He anticipated that, as a result, one day the human body would not be able to cope with the demands of the brain.[28]

In Zaydan's view, evolution and progress did not apply to the human body; very little physical change had occurred between the first men and twentieth-century man. Real evolution and progress took place in the fields of human morals and knowledge. This was the opposite of the case with animals. In humans, evolution has an impact on mental powers, while in animals the impact is on the anatomy. An unnamed author was quoted as saying that the human race will disappear as a result of social conditions that work against natural laws. Modern war seemed to be a primary factor that helped to keep alive unfit men and women (who would presumably die if left to natural factors) while the fit were the ones to vanish. In this light, Zaydan concluded that the idea of natural selection could be called reverse selection.[29] The author expressed his discontent with certain writers who used the concept of struggle for survival to justify war.

Zaydan found Henry Drummond among the best expositors of the importance of co-operation in life. In his book, *The Ascent of Man*, where he dealt with the struggle for life, Drummond emphasized that love, co-operation, and friendship are also laws of nature and are necessary for evolution in all living organisms. In nature there are laws regulating the survival of others which are as important as the laws of struggle for survival of the self. The author illustrated his point by noting that when one looks at a drop of water under a microscope, many small living organisms with one cell can be seen performing two functions. One is alimentation, the other is cellular reproduction. He maintained that the first process is based on self-interest and the second represents altruism and sacrifice for the survival of the species.[30] He also quoted Friedrich Schiller, the German poet, who said that the world walks on two feet – food and love. The first gave life to individuals in the species and the second gave life to an entire social community. Zaydan concluded his remarks by emphasizing the positive aspects of human evolution and progress. The more man progresses and evolves, the more he co-operates and sacrifices himself, the less selfish and self-indulgent he becomes.[31]

As one might expect, Musa explained his views on this matter in an article entitled 'Nazaa Jadida fi al-Ilm min al-Maddiyya ila al-Rohiyyah' (The New Movement in Science: From Materialism to Spiritualism).[32] He felt sorry for German materialism which had led to the unholy war. Like Sarruf, Musa agreed that 'Germany drank from materialism until it poisoned her body and then rushed, when she was at the height of material insanity, into this ugly war'.[33] Musa added that the death of Ernst Haeckel, in 1919, deprived the world of perhaps the last among the leaders of materialists. Musa argued that scientists at this time were advocating contrary views to those held by their ancestors, that spirit is the origin of matter. And this new movement, to him, manifested itself in a great deal of research on spiritualism. Musa considered Darwin's views as the demarcation between the old and the new. He argued that Darwin's work produced in Germany, the traditional land of idealism (Kant, Schopenhauer and Nietzsche), a sudden change to materialism in science, literature and industry. The Germans, moreover, became the principal expositors of the new principles.[34]

Musa referred to the late nineteenth-century debate on whether function brought organs into being or whether organs caused the creation of function: did vision follow the appearance of eyes, or did the appearance of eyes create vision? In Musa's view, function came before form: 'Life is a collection of functions or obligations, and body is a sum total of organs.' Life came before organism.

> If life or existence preceded the body or structure, then life is immortal. It does not depend on personification and it will continue after the disappearance of the body.[35]

Life lay at the centre of Schopenhauer's work; it was the force in Bernard Shaw's ideas; spirit reigned in Bergson's writings.

Musa concluded his article by emphasizing that the importance of this new school of spiritualism lay in diminishing materialistic competition. It drew the attention of world leaders to the spiritual needs of man. The difference between a man and an ape was the difference between their anatomy, not their souls (*ruh*). The soul was immortal and expressed itself through the body where it created vital organs. Musa maintained that the force of superman resides in each person. One had a duty to help the spirit by breeding those with the best bodies.[36]

Musa also commented on Arthur Keith, the British biologist, who had spoken on war and the survival of the fittest in 1930. He rejected Keith's claim that war was the best method for the survival of the fittest and that hatred between human races prevent inter-marriage, thereby encouraging natural selection.[37] (Keith had argued that the creation of the League of Nations was a step backward, since it hindered nature from its progress towards the survival of the fittest.)

In Musa's view, man in his secondary social behaviour puts human interest ahead of purely natural behaviour. Nature calls for struggle and the destruction of the weak, while humanity demands co-operation and treatment of the sick and weak. The League of Nations is for co-operation and mutual help but war is for struggle. Musa continued that the League's function resembles the role played by medicine or other human inventions that work against nature.[38] Musa's refutation of the principle of natural selection and the survival of the fittest was based on human reason, not on scientific grounds. If the struggle for survival were applied to modern human conditions, then people would live naked, abolish medical treatment for the sick and allow war to take place. Although war could lead to the victory of strong nations, it still acted as a counterproductive force because it killed the most fit among the nation's youth. But Musa saw no reason for humanity to follow this inhumane path. Man's vision improved his living conditions; he formulated new laws which were superior to natural laws. In this way, men would eventually discover how to avoid war and hatred. The best example of this evolution, according to Musa, was the recent trend among many civilized nations to prevent the unfit or the handicapped members of society from marrying and procreating. In this way, one could replace violence and destruction of nature by humane policies.[39]

In another article in the same issue of *al-Majalla al-Jadida* of 1930, Musa discussed in detail the aims of European and American efforts to sterilize the unfit.[40] He explained the policies of the Eugenics Society.

Some religious leaders in England, he noted, like Birmingham's bishop, not only advised people to heed the society's recommendation but also emphasized the necessity of sterilization among the handicapped. Musa repeated Shaw's argument in favour of eugenics.

One Arab version of natural selection came from Hafiz Mahmud, who wrote a short article entitled 'Al-Intikhab al-Ijtimai' (Social Selection) which appeared in the first year of *al-Majalla al-Jadida*, in 1929.[41] Mahmud suggested that scientists had constructed a law called natural selection to explain how nature selected the fittest social systems. He called this procedure the theory of social selection, and felt that it was more evident than the natural one. He explained that natural selection is an extremely slow process, while social selection occurs quickly. It took only a few years before a social system dramatically changed or evolved. He provided Noah's flood as an example of the beginning of the new social system: the flood destroyed most of the earth's population and left only a few unharmed. From the return of the earth of Noah's descendants, new societies began. The rise and fall of the Pharaonic and Roman empires and the Greek city states were also due to social evolution.[42]

One of the most sophisticated Arab analyses of the law of struggle for survival came from Ismail Mazhar. Mazhar began an article entitled 'Al-Tanahur Ala al-Baqa' (The Struggle for Survival) applying Darwin's doctrine by focusing on social scientists.[43] These scientists, he wrote, misinterpreted the concept of the struggle for survival. The socialists (*al-Ijtimaiyun*) took this concept at its face value and used it as if it were refined truth. Mazhar provided the example of Nietzsche's philosophy in Germany, Nietzsche's superman.[44] This is the man who eventually will win the battle of life or the struggle for survival. Mazhar abhorred seeing racial discrimination and material attainments based only on strength. He emphasized that these realities would not last long.

It is no surprise, therefore, that Mazhar gave full support to Peter Kropotkin, the Russian biologist of 'mutual aid'. Mazhar thought that Kropotkin applied Darwin's theory correctly. Kropotkin admitted, according to Mazhar, that the struggle for survival among species in fact indicated a struggle against an adverse environment. Mutual aid governed livings organisms.

This is exactly what Darwin had warned: The concept of struggle for existence was used in a metaphoric sense and cannot be applied as it appears in a literal sense.[45]

Mazhar also cited Walter Bagehot, who published a book on physics and politics. Bagehot explained that human struggle is based on intelligence or mental superiority. Happy to find that Kropotkin's and Bagehot's work represented a congenial interpretation of Darwin's ideas, Mazhar concluded, 'we need not only to define scientific concepts properly, but, more importantly, to understand the real meaning of the ideas'.[46] He criticized a public figure in the Egyptian Ministry of Education, who did not provide the right interpretation. The figure – perhaps, Ismail Hasanayn, who was Deputy Minister of Education of Egypt in 1923 – advocated that Darwin's teaching encouraged racial conflicts and that the world would end with only one race. One could anticipate annihilation of the coloured races such as those in America and Australia.

Two years later, Mazhar wrote an essay and delivered a speech on the theory of evolution and developed his own interpretation of the struggle for life. The essay bore the title 'Min Baqa al-Aslah Ila Baqa al-Atlah' (From the Survival of the Fittest to the Survival of the Unfit) and appeared in *al-Usur*, Mazhar's own journal in 1930.[47] In this essay, instead of discussing the causes for the survival of the unfit, as Musa had done successfully, Mazhar examined how social scientists like Bagehot and Kropotkin applied Darwin's theory to their work. Influenced by Kropotkin, Mazhar tried to prove that the real meaning of natural selection was not the victory of the strongest and the most violent but co-operation and mutual aid among individuals.[48] Mazhar cited the struggle between religion and science in late nineteenth-century Europe. He recounted the story of the Spanish doctor, Gregorio Chil y Naranjo, who published a study on the natural history of the Canary Islands in 1878.[49] In this study, Chil examined Darwin's theory in the light of his findings in the islands and seemed to support it. This study helped diffuse Darwin's ideas and was a clear challenge to Catholic Spain.

The main corpus of Mazhar's interpretation and analysis of the law of struggle for survival came in his address at the first annual meeting of the Egyptian Society for Scientific Culture in March of 1930. The speech, entitled 'Al-Tatawwur wa Atharuh fi Mustaqbal al-Fikr al-Insani'[50] (Evolution and Its Impact on the Future of Human Thought), largely consisted of repetition. Mazhar advanced four connected but distinguishable cases relating to the struggle. First 'Al-Tanahur al-Aksi' (Reversal Struggle), a struggle against natural elements or factors, when a living organism resists temperature, cold and other factors. Second is 'Al-Tanahur al-Ijabi' (Positive Struggle), a struggle for food, when the living organism benefits from things which could substitute loss of vital force in resistance of natural elements. Third is 'Al-Tanahur al-Takafuyi' (Reward Struggle), a struggle where a living organism attempts to obtain as much as it can from the equilibrium between its structure and the surrounding environment.[51] Fourth is 'Al-Tanahur al-Tadili' (Collective Struggle), a struggle for collectivity where individual living organisms adjust themselves to accommodate to the needs of the group. Using these cases, Mazhar gave his own answers to social problems. The first image of struggle provides a sense of beauty and religious feeling; the second produces economic life; the third produces high morals like will-power and self-guidance; while the last struggle maintains the social fabric of the higher species.[52]

Discussion of the meaning of Darwin's concepts was furthered through a series of articles by Ismail Hasanayn Basha, Deputy Minister of Education in Egypt, entitled 'Al-Taawun wa al-Taalim' (Co-operation and Education) which appeared in *al-Muqtataf* in 1923.[53] The author criticized as irrelevant the education provided to Egyptian students. He added that an educational system saturated with Darwin's and Nietzsche's theories credits only those strengths which promote the struggle for survival and does not encourage good character and brotherhood.[54] The time had therefore come for schools to suppress such ideologies and promote a principle that provides for co-operation and generosity.

In a letter to *al-Muqtataf*, Mazhar completely rejected Hasanayn's arguments on Darwin's principles.[55] Nature is never a bloody battle, he argued, where the strong kills the weak. He asked:

When, at any time in history, have the principles of education provided people with good character and brotherhood? When could Darwin's theory of the struggle for survival be the cause for man to acquire an animalistic character? . . . This is Plato's Republic, a well known work, and it was the source for teaching in the Middle Ages. It did not provide man with morals and brotherhood before Darwin.[56]

Indeed, Mazhar argued, words like brotherhood, freedom and equality cannot be the basis for scientific discussion. Darwin's principle of the survival of the fittest simply produces successful men, and these men are the result of inherited factors. Education was not an issue. Mazhar concluded his reply by claiming that there must be a distinction between the social or educational theories on one side and natural laws on the other. He advised the Egyptian Minister to read Bagehot and Kropotkin on the meaning of the struggle for the survival of the fittest in the theory of evolution.[57] It was not his intention, Mazhar added, to defend Nietzsche, who exaggerated the application of Darwin's principles. Rather, he defended the great teacher Darwin against those who misused his ideas.

5 Traditionalist Responses to Darwinism

INTRODUCTION

This section discusses the conflict over Darwin and revelation that was mainly conducted between Sarruf on the one hand and Louis Cheikho, the editor of *al-Mashriq*, and Ibrahim al-Yaziji, the editor of *al-Diya*, on the other.[1] As we will see, the Arab thinkers used Scripture to support their arguments. While Darwin's *Origin of Species* made almost no reference to humankind, the publication of the *The Descent of Man* sparked a bitter conflict between religious opinion and evolutionary ideas. As in the West, Arab religious groups adhered to the literal truth of the word of God in the Bible. Louis Cheikho was perhaps the most prominent among the Christian Arabs to counter any challenge to religious opinion.

Arab Christian groups, including Catholic, Protestant and Orthodox, had many sources for defending their traditional faith. Among these sources were the translation into Arabic of Western writings and the return of students from Europe. Christian periodicals like the Jesuit journals *al-Mashriq* and *al-Bashir* and the Protestant periodical *al-Nashra al-Usbuiyya*, defended the religious point of view. The journals were not above internecine and sectarian discussions. Protestants were forcefully attacked by Catholic propagandists and *vice versa*. Cheikho and other writers for *al-Mashriq*, for example, contested religious and scientific issues with *al-Hilal*, *al-Muqtataf*, *al-Diya* and sometimes *al-Jamiat*. The Muslim periodicals, however, mainly *al-Manar* and *al-Irfan*, were treated with extreme care by Christian editors. There were few direct attacks on Islam, all such being conducted in an amicable manner.[2]

With this exception, debates were conducted with harsh language in a sarcastic and acrimonious manner. Cheikho's was the prototype of this style of polemical writing. He often directed his attacks at people by name. Cheikho upheld traditional views on the question of

64

animal intelligence, man's creation, the manna of the Jews, science and religion, the origin and mystery of life, St Augustine's doctrine, spontaneous generation of life, and the rotation of the earth. Yet, Cheikho's style did nothing to restrain the interest of Arab secularists in exploring and popularizing the subject of evolution.

ANIMAL INTELLIGENCE

One of the issues discussed in Darwin's *Descent of Man* was the origin of the moral and intellectual nature of man. He attributed this origin to a gradual modification and development from lower animals. The exhibition of intelligence and reasoning power, as well as the use of means to attain ends, are present in animals just as they are in man. Examples of curiosity, imitation, imagination, memory, consciously knowing right from wrong and social and moral qualities in animals were interpreted by Darwinists as evidence of compassion, pride and shame. Animals had 'language'. They had the ability to count and remember numbers. There was much debate in the Arab world over the implications of animal intelligence. This issue was a source of controversy between Arab secularists and religious men, especially the Christians. Arab secularists sought to bring to the attention of Arab readers some of the biological and moral relationships between animals and humans. Their writings did not lend support to the notion of a special creation of the human species, as revealed in religious texts.

One of the earliest debates on the question of animal intelligence came after the appearance of an article under the title 'Al-Quwa al-Aqila Fi al-Hayawan' (On Animal Rational Power), which appeared in *al-Diya* in 1899. This article, written by Khalil Saad, echoed the views on animal reasoning which were discussed by Western writers.[3] In a reply to Saad, Father Cheikho attacked the materialists' attempts to provide biological or physiological equality between man and animal.[4] He quoted Psalms 48:12, 'And yet earthling man, though in honour, cannot keep lodging; He is indeed comparable with the beasts that have been destroyed.'[5] This verse was interpreted to mean that 'humans who cannot comprehend' resemble animals that had no reason. Cheikho saw Saad attempting to place animals above man. He questioned what Saad meant by his title 'Animal Reasoning'. If animals had the ability to reason, then nothing distinguished man from beasts. In time, animals could evolve and progress to reach man's level. This was plainly absurd, in Cheikho's view. Animal traits like curiosity, imitation, attention and comprehension could not be called rational or intelligent (*aqila*) but rather instinctive (*gharizah*). Instincts peculiar to animals were called by some philosophers (he did not mention their names), the 'imaginary powers (*al-quwa al-wahimah*).[6] Cheikho also took issue with Saad on the morals of animals. Cheikho considered these morals as mere human inventions without existence. What 'we observe from animal acts does not demonstrate more than a mere primitive and animalistic feeling'.[7] As a concluding note, Cheikho expressed his abhorrence of the last paragraph of Saad's article where 'reason or rationality is a common concept which can be applied to all kinds of animals, including man, who shares with animals certain feelings and characteristics'.[8]

In a rejoinder to Cheikho, Saad praised the Jesuits for their work in the service of the nation and science.[9] He went on to defend his views on animal intelligence on both scientific and religious grounds. From the religious point of view, Saad noted that even if the Holy Book did not give animals reason or the intelligence to comprehend things, both animals and humans had one common faculty. To support his argument, Saad quoted the old Biblical story in Genesis on the snake's tempting Eve with the forbidden fruit of knowledge. In this light, Saad wrote:

> An animal that tempted the first woman could possess reason or intelligence greater than other animals and still be created by God.[10]

Saad's scientific defence was based on challenging Cheikho to provide a demarcation between instinct and reason. If Cheikho did so, Saad would be ready to introduce many cases where animals conducted themselves in a manner that made humans seem base. Saad emphasized the unity of reason between both animals and humans by referring to a child raised in an area where he was isolated from other humans but where he had access to hearing animal's voices and their movement. This child, Saad asserted, would grow to act like any other animal in the area. Therefore, Saad asked, 'What is the difference in this case between the child and animal except in certain characteristics that are inherited from the child's parents?'[11] In conclusion, Saad acknowledged his ignorance of the real causes that hindered the progress of animals to a level where they could compete with humans. The ants, he said, performed certain acts that puzzled the philosophers and some still cannot accept the reason that lies behind such intelligent acts.

This clear indication of Saad's religious convictions did not silence Cheikho, who had to have the final word. He did not accept Saad's quotation from Psalms and declared that the scriptural passage provides only for a fundamental difference between man and animal. He added that if a human does not comply with the word of God, he becomes like an animal; man should use his reason, if he wants to be distinguished from the brutes, by knowing the will of God.[12] As to Saad's assertion that the Bible affirmed the unity of reason between man and brute animals, Cheikho delivered a refutation on logical rather than on biblical grounds. Sarcastic in his attack, he labelled Saad as a Christian by name, but as one who never read or believed in the Bible; then he wrote that the example of the snake in Eden made him laugh. While Cheikho seems, indirectly, to deny the snake's ability to speak, he asked:

If the snake spoke so, why, today, have snakes forgotten their ancestor's language? Did not the law of evolution and progress claim that the origin of man and beast came from a small germ that evolved with time to reach the present stage of development?[13]

Here Cheikho's reliance on logic rather than the Bible to support his debate can be considered a new departure. As to Saad's scientific argument, Cheikho declared that while he accepted the idea of animal intelligence, he refused to accept any evidence for the existence of animal reason. Saad did not reply. In another short article, Cheikho claimed that logical evidence in support of man's special status on earth had silenced Saad. He labelled Saad's ideas as non-religious, even rotten, and followed this with a religious proclamation to forbid Catholics from reading *al-Diya*.[14]

The debate on animal intelligence continued in the pages of *al-Diya* between Father Qustantin and Saad.[15] While maintaining his old stand on the issue of animal rationality, Saad asserted that he did not posit an equality between man and animal, since the lowest human savage had a rational and moral power superior to that of the highest monkeys.[16] He added that even if the Holy Book gave no rationality or intelligence to animals, the mental or rational principle was a common heritage among both man and animal. In Saad's view, the supporters of the evolution theory believed that the unit of the mind or mental principle (*al-Mabda al-Aqli*) can be found among all living creatures. Under the influence of certain environmental conditions, some animals had the capacity to use their forefeet. This use was enhanced by the necessity of encompassing many actions and deeds, eventually leading some animals to surpass the development of other animals and later reach the stage of total cognitive power, which distinguished them from animals whose comprehension was fractional. This partial comprehension was called by Saad instinct (*gharizat*) or imaginary power (*al-quwa al-aqila*).[17]

Arab writing on animal intelligence was obviously intended to provide support to Darwin's theory of evolution by bridging the gap between humans and animals. In other words, apart from the physiological and biological similarities that existed between man and lower animals, there also existed a psychic relation between the two. The drama of animal intelligence or instinct cannot be discussed at length here.[18] What concerns us in this study is to point out the conscious efforts made by Arab secularists to incorporate and popularize the wider ramifications of Darwin's ideas before Eastern Arab readers.

HOLY WATER, THE STAR OF BETHLEHEM, MANNA AND THE HUMAN SOUL

As a Catholic, Cheikho considered the scientific writings of his main adversaries, the editors of *al-Muqtataf* and *al-Hilal*, as spurious and not truly scientific.[19] The editors of these journals had the obvious advantage that they were trained in science, while Cheikho had no formal education in any scientific subjects. Cheikho freely admitted his lack of scientific background, but he refused to accept *al-Muqtataf's* claim that *al-Mashriq* was unqualified to treat scientific topics. In his own words:

> Our journal, exactly as theirs, is scientific, literary and artistic, in spite of the owner's apparent lack of deep knowledge in certain scientific fields. Nonetheless he is only one of many contributors who, thanks to God, represent every branch of knowledge, and the journal draws upon their expertise. In addition, they have access to more than 150 different periodicals in all European languages. Therefore, the editor can follow scientific development just as the owners of *al-Muqtataf* can, both of whom carry the title Doctor of Philosophy.[20]

He further accused the editors of mixing science with philosophy because they attributed to science certain results that are based on unfounded philosophical and value judgements.[21] Some of these issues concern the contamination of holy water with microbes, the discovery of the sap of the tamarisk in the desert of Sinai and the manna of the exodus. They will be discussed in turn.

After Sarruf and Nimr examined holy water in some churches, they found that it was contaminated with various germs that caused colds and diphtheria. This simple scientific statement was reported in *al-Muqtataf's* section of scientific news.[22] Not denying the scientific validity of the claim, Cheikho asserted that the holy water was the same as any water, except that it was blessed and salted by the priests. He maintained that if microbes were found in it, it was not because the water was holy, but because it was taken from an infected area.[23] Again Cheikho's sarcastic style was evident when he said that the 'killer microbes found in the holy water' were meant for 'al-Abalisah' (devils) meaning of course, Sarruf and Nimr.[24]

In the Christian Arab reception of Western science, modern science appeared as a tool to reinforce traditional beliefs and faiths. In the first year of *al-Mashriq*, an article appeared under the heading 'The Meteors and the Star of the Magi' ('al-Nayazik wa Najm al-Majusi'), written by Father Sebastian Rinzval, a Jesuit.[25] In his search to provide scientific evidence for the Star of Bethlehem, he sketched the historical appearance of meteors (or, as he used the French term, *étoiles filantes*) from the time of the ancient Greeks until the present. Without mentioning his sources, he quoted the work of Chladni, the German naturalist, and Howard, the British chemist, on the number of meteors, or aerolites, that had fallen on the earth from 1478 BC to AD 1794. He said, the fall of an aerolite to the earth was finally accepted after the French scientist, Biot, submitted his findings on the subject to the Paris Academy of Sciences in 1803. But why did scientists not accept this phenomenon until 1803? The author replied that 'corrupt science attempted to contradict the Word of God'.[26] He quoted Joshua 10:11:

And it came about that while they were fleeing from before Israel and were on the descent of Beth-horon, Jehovah hurled great stones from the heavens upon them as far as Azekah, so that they died. There were more who died from the hail stones than those whom the sons of Israel killed with swords.[27]

The writer asserted that the philosophers of the eighteenth century denied this statement but that modern science itself explained the error of their claim. He insisted that 'real sciences do not contradict but always support holy writings'.[28]

As for the Star of Bethlehem, his main concern, Father Rinzval had no idea about its exact nature. He mentioned three possibilities: first, it was like a star that came near the earth by an act of God; second, it was a meteor; and third, it was a normal star. As expected, the Jesuit sided with the first opinion which advocated that God miraculously created the star to guide the Magi to the birthplace of Jesus, contrary to natural laws. In a footnote he cited another Jesuit paper, *al-Bashir*, in 1884, which provided support for the miracle of the Magi. In his conclusion he quoted a paragraph of Newton's letter to another scientist in which Newton referred to the need for heavenly guidance on the rotation of the stars around the sun.

As part of his campaign to vindicate the reality of divine miracles, Cheikho confronted *al-Muqtataf* on the manna of the Israelites. In a letter to *al-Mashriq*, an anonymous person had demanded an explanation for the controversy surrounding the nature of the manna. Cheikho blamed *al-Muqtataf's* editors for disseminating 'the poison of doubt and atheist teachings' among the populace.[29] After quoting the biblical version of the nature and colour of the manna as described in Exodus 16:4, 5, 14–32 and Numbers 11:7, Cheikho appealed to readers who believed in the Old Testament to judge for themselves if it were possible to interpret these biblical verses in a natural way that contradicted God's work and his miracles. Cheikho maintained that God's miraculous production of the manna proved his love of the Israelites.[30] *Al-Muqtataf* had reported that many trees produced a liquid or juice that resembled the manna of the Bible. Cheikho completely rejected *al-Muqtataf's* allegations on the new discovery of the plant juice in the desert of Sinai. In his effort to differentiate between the Israelites' manna and the new manna, Cheikho appealed to the miracles and the words of the Bible.[31] He provided a historical sketch of all studies conducted on the trees and plants that produce the modern manna. He found that modern manna was neither in a quantity sufficient to feed the Israelites even for one day nor was it suitable by itself for human consumption.[32] Cheikho argued that the biblical manna had a unique characteristic which clearly distinguished it from the modern material. It appeared unexpectedly on a daily basis for immediate consumption, for it would decay if left over for the following day, with the exception of

Saturday, the Israelite's day of rest, as commanded by God.[33] According to Cheikho, the fact that the manna did not appear on Saturday was undeniably the symbol of a miracle. Acting as a winner in this debate, Cheikho concluded by asserting that the non-believers who denied these miracles and did not accept the great difference between the divine manna and the newly discovered one had failed in their efforts.[34]

Although Cheikho expressed his dissatisfaction with almost all of the subjects which appeared in the 1898 issues of *al-Muqtataf* (including a translation into Arabic of some of Herbert Spencer's work) he decided to refute only one of them. Cheikho wrote on 'Ray al-Muqtataf fi al-Aql al-Bashari' (*Al-Muqtataf's* Opinion on the Human Mind) in which he accused *al-Muqtataf* of defending materialism and supporting what he called Darwin's inventions.[35] One of many points that Cheikho refuted was the question of the human intellect. The editor of *al-Muqtataf* defined the term as:

> The sum total of brain and nerves whether the organism senses it or not; the body of every animal, higher or lower, including humans, consisted of organs which perform certain functions . . . the most sophisticated of these organs are those located in the head. Thus, the brain is like a machine and the mind is its function and both progress and regress together.[36]

Cheikho explained that *al-Muqtataf's* editors set out to show that the difference between man and animals is the fact that animals are completely under the influence of external circumstances; the ones which survive are those that can adapt to changing conditions. Animal actions become mechanical and gradually develop into instincts. As for humans, with time and effort, mental capacity increased and the ability to distinguish between good and evil grew, while beasts lived and died according to their instincts. In his reply, Cheikho wrote:

> If this is proven, the basis of humanity will collapse, and humans will be placed at the same level as beasts. If the latter found a suitable environment, with vigorous efforts they could reach the stage of man.[37]

Cheikho sought to refute the materialistic interpretation of universe and life. He felt that after the soul leaves the body, it continues to live, but without brain and nerves. The mind is not the total sum of brain and nerve action as *al-Muqtataf* claimed. That *al-Muqtataf* confined the definition of mind was corrupt in the first place, because it did not take into consideration the totality of mental characteristics and did not differentiate between the human mind and the mind of lower animals, since the latter had brains and nerves as well. Therefore, Cheikho insisted that the editors of *al-Muqtataf*, by always trying to inject some reasoning ability into animals, were only bending facts to serve Darwinism.[38] Cheikho still considered Darwinism an illusionary collection of unproven facts. In a footnote, Cheikho drew the reader's attention to work published by three anti-Darwinian Arab writers who subscribed to beliefs similar to Cheikho's. These writers were Jurjis Faraj, al-Afghani and Ibrahim al-Hourani.[39]

Eager to provide the right definition for mind, Cheikho claimed that his definition was based on that of true and honest philosophers. 'Mind is a force completely separated from matter, through which humans understand the nature of things.'[40] While the brain is material and divided up into cells, he wrote, the mind is separate from matter and nothing can confine or limit it; mind is one unit and can move from the upper part of the sky to the lowest point beneath the earth. Mind can comprehend the invisible existence of god, moral duties and religion. Influenced by ancient Arab philosophers, he referred his opponents to Ibn Miskawayh's work on the subject.[41]

One aspect of the question of mind revolved around the claim of the naturalists that mind increases with the increase of brain, and *vice versa.* Cheikho asserted that this conclusion provides that mind could replace the function of brain in the case of mental disorders occuring as a consequence of brain damage. Although admitting that the brain is essential to mind and any injury to the former might affect the latter, Cheikho insisted on a separate function for each. The mind is also comparable, according to Cheikho, to a worker whose need for tools is essential; the worker and his tools are in no way equivalent.[42]

While still in its first year of publication *al-Mashriq* challenged another secularist journal and its editor. The journal was *al-Hilal*, owned by Jurji Zaydan. Cheikho looked at the specific arguments of *al-Hilal's* editor and tried to refute them one by one. One of his earliest encounters with Zaydan was over two questions: the immortality of the human soul, and Adam as the father of mankind. In a letter to the editor, Niquula Ghattas, a priest, asked if certain current views were compatible with traditional religious beliefs on the immortality of human soul. In reply, Zaydan wrote an article on the subject, entitled 'Ma Hiya al-Nafs al-Bashariyah wa-Sifatuha wa-Masdaruha wa-Masiruha' (The Nature of Human Soul: Its Characteristics, Its Origin and Its Final Destiny).[43] In it, Zaydan declined to discuss religious matters, especially the sensitive question of the soul. He asserted that the question of the soul's immortality was a controversial one and no consensus had yet been reached on it among philosophers. Cheikho claimed that only false and dishonest philosophers like Rousseau and Voltaire, whom Zaydan cited, rejected the notion of the human soul. He promoted other philosophers who based their argument on 'sound reasons', men like Ibn Sina (Avicenna) and St Thomas Aquinas. Again here Cheikho used the words 'rational' and 'reason' to discredit Zaydan's argument on the religious meaning of the soul. While Cheikho believed that religion provided support for the notion of the soul, he insisted, as a good Jesuit would insist, that through reason and rational discussion one could come to the same conclusion as through faith.

Cheikho also addressed Zaydan's writings on the biblical Adam. He wrote an article under the same heading, 'Adam Abu al-Bashar' (Adam Is The Father of Mankind), in which Cheikho reminded Zaydan not to discuss religious matters which were beyond his competence.[44] Zaydan had wanted to give scientific proofs that contradicted the story of Adam as related by the Bible. According to some scientists, Adam was not the first man created on the earth because when one compared the age of Creation with the law of natural evolution, the interval of time claimed from scripture was not enough to explain the growth and evolution of nations and governments.[45] To this, Cheikho asserted that the Church provided neither for a specific age of the universe nor for the elapsed time since Adam's creation. Even Catholic scientists provided different calculations of mankind's age. This range in calculations could serve to accommodate modern scientific discoveries, and there was no need therefore, to advocate that Adam was not the father of mankind. Cheikho's acceptance, even indirectly, of Zaydan's version of the story constituted a new departure in his attitude toward scientific facts.[46]

In its second year, *al-Mashriq* published an article by the Bishop of Antioch, Girmanous Muaqqad, entitled 'Al-Ilm al-Haqiqi' (The True Science).[47] In his article, the Bishop was concerned with the problem of separating true science from practical science (*sinaat*). The author asserted that grammar, rhetoric and languages were not sciences while logic and other branches of philosophy were the genuine article. The latter sciences not only led to the discovery of nature's secrets but also provided for natural morals and duties of the individual towards himself and towards God.[48] The bishop attempted to find a rough distinction between true and untrue science. This can be considered the first attempt by an Arab religious leader to differentiate between science and the uses or application of it.

Another Jesuit, Father Louis Renzval, devoted a lengthy article to explain the concept of animal instinct, 'Fi al-Wahimah wa-al-Gharizah' (On the Imaginative Faculty and Instinct in Animals).[49] It appeared in *al-Mashriq* in 1901. There the author attempted to define what he considered the inventive intelligence of animals. The definition was 'a power that enables the beasts to comprehend or understand certain acts, be they good or bad, that other senses cannot detect'.[50] While the author differentiated between the uses of imaginative and instinctual intelligence, he maintained that instinct was more commonly used by animals.

Renzval's discussion of the subject was not accidental. He devoted the entire article to refuting those aspects of Darwin's evolutionary thought which did not provide for a special creation for man. He wrote that the primitive and instinctual behaviour of animals in their ability to act for a purpose but without prior intention was possible due to divine wisdom acting through instinct. As expected, the author also placed emphasis on the necessity of introducing a new word to describe the equivalent of instinct in man. He noted that in the case of man the drive of instinct was not as strong as in animals. According to Renzval, Darwin and Spencer incorrectly claimed that in evolution and transformation we see constant repetition elevated to instinct.[51] This repetition of acts eventually became an acquired characteristic. This strange explanation, Renzval emphasized, was based on pure imagination and unproven facts. That a hound has the inclination to hunt and a sharp sense of smell led the Darwinists to believe that some habits are genetically inherited. Animals, however, could not acquire these unnatural inclinations without training from man.[52] These inclinations would not persist if man stopped his husbandry. Like many of the writers, among them Cheikho, Renzval confused Lamarck's ideas on acquired characteristics with those of Darwin on natural selection and survival of the fittest.

Not only did Cheikho refute articles or reports on evolutionary theory and its defence by Arab secularists, but he also concerned himself with any other works that contained 'the poison of Darwinism'. Under the subtitle 'Darwiniyyat al-Muqtataf' (al-Muqtataf's Darwinism) in the *Shazarat* section of *al-Mashriq*, Cheikho attacked an article that had appeared in *al-Muqtataf* on astronomical ins-truments.[53] The editor of *al-Muqtataf* reported that the human eye was simple in its structure and function; with time it evolved, and in the future the eye would evolve to an even more advanced stage. Another report on the structure of the eye appeared in *al-Hilal* which argued that in the past man had three eyes, had recently lost one, and in the near future would be left only with one eye. The articles in *al-Muqtataf* and *al-Hilal* were simply summaries of recent studies without mention of authors' names. Happy to find that both editors failed to publish the names of those scientists who wrote the original articles, Cheikho wondered which of these scientists the journals drew to produce such a contradictory view on the human eye.

Cheikho's defence of religion went beyond the Arab East. He also was aware of Arab writings in North and South America. He devoted a lengthy discussion to the refutation of what he called 'Al-Fatawi al-Amrikyya Fi al-Mutaqadat al-Dinyya' (American Proclamations on Religious Beliefs), in which he attacked two Arab journals, one published in New York and the other in Sao Paulo, Brazil.[54]

The first was *al-Jamiah*, a secularist periodical founded in 1899 by Farah Antun in Cairo, who later moved to New York. Antun wrote an article on the animal mind which appeared in his journal in 1909. In it, he mentioned how animals could reason just as human beings. He provided some striking data on three cats which developed reasoning powers. The cats could apparently distinguish numbers written on their food dishes. Antun mentioned other species' capacity for intelli-gent action: a horse that answered his master's questions by knocking his hoof on the ground to denote numerical dates, and a monkey's intentional action in building houses. The author introduced Dar-win's thought as proven fact. Cheikho was dismayed with Antun's absolute certainty about Darwin's findings and considered his praise of animal mind as evidence of a pro-Darwinist attitude. Without providing any rational criticism, Cheikho repeated his style of violent language. Far from seeking a rapprochement with Arab secularists, he referred Antun to Louis Renzval's ideas on animal instinct.

Cheikho also attacked Milham K. Abduh and Kais Lipky, the latter being editor of *al-Hadiqat* in Brazil.[55] Both Brazilian Arabs were of the opinion that religion and science were in conflict and a reconciliation between evolution and theology would be hard to achieve. Responding favourably to Spencer, Darwin and Renan, Abduh developed a lengthy discussion on religion and science. Most relevant to the present study was his assertion that religion needs to be adapted to the scientific spirit of the age, especially with respect to Darwin's theory of progress and evolution.[56] In his reply, Cheikho wrote that if what Abduh claimed was correct, then the scientific output of numerous writers, many of them priests and bishops, would be in doubt. He pointed out that Jesuits ran 14 major astronomical observatories around the world. The findings of men of faith were not discredited simply because they would not renounce religion.[57] Cheikho maintained that the refutation of evolution by men of faith was based not only on religious but also on scientific bases. He affirmed that many thinkers who did not have any religious affiliations found no convincing evidence in Darwin's doctrine.[58] Cheikho's disagreement with Lipky concerns the biblical story of Joshua. Lipky contended that this story was contrary to scientific laws. In reply, Cheikho referred Lipky to a study conducted by the Jesuits on the subject.[59]

As will be evident, a considerable part of Arab secularist writing was concerned with science, especially Darwin's theory and its relation to religion. A number of scientific opinions and discoveries could not be discussed fully in public, because they contradicted popular beliefs. Arab evolutionists possessed knowledge that was not directly accessible to more than a handful of intellectuals. Unlike in the case of Cheikho, their appeal to the Arab reading public aimed to present scientific facts rather than emotional polemics. One of the most interesting examples of this approach was Cheikho's reply to Zaydan's complaint against the traditional Arab attitude towards modern science, which I now discuss.

On various occasions Cheikho emphasized the unity of science and religion. He wrote a note under the title 'Rai al-Hilal fi al-Irtiqa' (Al-Hilal's Opinion on Evolution).[60] It was designed to refute Zaydan's accusation that traditional Arab views were antithetical to science. Zaydan had indicated that Arab writers did not have the liberty to discuss natural sciences, mention discoveries or advance unorthodox opinions that contradicted popular convictions. If one did so, Zaydan added, one would immediately be labelled as an atheist and ridiculed. Traditional-minded Arabs, Zaydan wrote, could not understand evolution. In his reply, Cheikho argued that Zaydan's assessment was unjustified. Happy to see Zaydan portray such an image of the Arab reading public, Cheikho took the occasion to praise his own journal and the other Jesuit paper, *al-Bashir*. He asserted that while both journals were chiefly concerned with the diffusion of modern and recent scientific development, they had never been labelled atheistic (*zandaqa*). He further explained that Eastern readers accepted only the scientific writings of journals that based their evidence on authentic sources. The author asked, did not Eastern readers have the right to verify the writings of those whose work, on many occasions, did not stand on good empirical evidence?[61]

Cheikho's indirect call to Arab readers to investigate the criteria provided by scientists seems to have been a genuine one. His call suggests that Cheikho was interested not so much in the course of scientific truth as in the issue of justification of knowledge, even that which was based on religious convictions. In his view, science and religion

are like twins, inseparable, and only the sinner would seek to separate them. Both science and religion came from one source, the order of the Prime Creator who controls everything in this world.[62]

There were, then, constraints on scientific evidence. This is exactly the line of thought adopted by Arab Muslim theologians, as we will see in the next chapter of this study.

In another article on the relation between science and religion, Cheikho went even further and declared, 'any religion that contradicts one scientific truth is a false religion'.[63] The same would also apply to any science that disproved a real religion.[64] Cheikho wrote the article to refute *al-Hilal's* allegation that in every religion – Judaism, Christianity or Islam – there are certain teachings in direct contradiction with natural facts. Zaydan quoted miracles as a case in point. In reply, Cheikho provided many biblical verses that not only encouraged scientific and religious investigation, but also urged men of religion to adopt scientific knowledge. He cited 'by knowledge are the righteous rescued' (Proverbs 11:9) and 'that the soul should be without knowledge, is not good' (Proverbs 19:2).[65] These verses, and others, were evidence to support his argument on the unity of science and religion. He also reiterated his earlier remarks on those men who had combined religion and science in their intellectual life, like St Augustine and St Thomas Aquinas from the religious side, and Cuvier, Ampère and Pasteur from the scientific side.

Another important theme raised by Arab modernists was that of the relationship between some members of the Church and the idea of evolution. They explained that one of the early Church Fathers, St

Augustine (354–430), was also one of the founders of the original idea
of Darwin's evolution. An article entitled 'Al-Qiddis Augustinus
wa-Namous al-Nushu wa al-Tahwwul' (St Augustine and the Law of
Evolution and Transformation) appeared in *al-Muqtataf* in 1913 by
Dr Amin Abu Khatir.[66] The essay was a translation of an old article
written by the French ideologue, Cabanis. Cabanis attempted to
demonstrate that religious men, if they really want to understand the
relationship between science and religion, should take the example of
the hermeneutical manner in which Augustine unfolded the con-
cealed facts of the Bible. Abu Khatir asserted that the doctrine of
evolution is basically contained in Augustine's idea on creation of
matter and its growth and evolution.[67] He further explained that St
Augustine provided proof of the concept of natural selection and
even supported the ideas of materialism. Abu Khatir stated that St
Augustine wrote that matter, which is the origin of all mechanical
and non-mechanical creatures, is inseparable from the force contained in it. Therefore, the author added, if Büchner had studied
Augustine's work, he would have added it to his stock of evidence.[68]
The direct attack by the Arab secularists constitutes a new approach
in the intellectual battle against Arab religious thinkers, who still
dominated the scene. It indicates a decline in religious resistance to
the introduction of modern scientific thought. This is by no means to
suggest that the vigour of debate under the leadership of Cheikho
had subsided, but rather to draw attention to the new offensive
strategy adopted by Arab secularists. They surely implemented the
new strategy in part to cause embarrassment for Cheikho, who
promoted the Bible and religious teaching as the absolute standards
for human thought.

Cheikho responded to Abu Khatir in an article entitled 'Al-Qiddis
Augustinus Shafi al-Madhab al-Darwini' (St Augustine, the Interces-
sor of Darwinian Doctrine) which appeared in *al-Mashriq* in 1913.[69]
In a less forceful and less convincing argument, he asserted that
Augustine's work had already been studied and understood by church-
men. For the first time, Cheikho mentioned some weaknesses in the
saint's writings, but he labelled Cabanis as one of the eighteenth
century atheists and materialists. He was happy to see St Augustine
as a forerunner of Darwin.[70]

At first, Cheikho's attention was directed against Darwin's ideas
on natural selection and survival of the fittest, which he dismissed as
unsound. The explanation was not difficult to find. He drew on the
writings of those who challenged some of Darwin's views on scientific

grounds, which were already known in the West. Among those were St George Mivart and Louis Agassiz. Cheikho seemed to avoid quoting the arguments provided by Wilberforce, an Anglican bishop, and Rufail Hawawini, an Orthodox bishop in Syria, to discredit Darwinism and materialism. No doubt Cheikho sought to stick to approved religious authorities.

After refuting Darwin's principle of natural selection, Cheikho went on to compare and contrast Augustine's thought with that of Darwin. He found that Abu Khatir had misrepresented Augustine's ideas by translating only 3 out of 265 pages of his book. Augustine was really in agreement with Church teaching and in disagreement with evolutionists.[71] Cheikho asserted that the saint believed that the creation of creatures by God resembled the 'small seed which contains in it the roots, branches and flowers of a tree'.[72] According to Cheikho, this statement was interpreted by some people to mean that species evolved from each other. They were mistaken.

The germ-plasm of this universe has a limited force and special characteristic which differentiate among every and each germ. . . and as such the wheat seeds do not produce beans and the seeds of beans do not yield wheat. Therefore, animals could not produce humans or man evolve from animals.[73]

In another open attack on Arab secularists, Father Yusuf al-Amshiti wrote an article entitled 'Al-Iman wa-al-Ilm Ikhwan la Yakhtalifan' (On the Unity of Science and Faith) which was published in *al-Mashriq* in 1923.[74] Al-Amshiti sought not to refute ideas or defend religion but to expose some Arab scholars who attached great weight to certain ideas that had already been discredited in the West. He listed scientists who praised the Lord's power to create: J. B. Dumas, Cauchy, Tycho Brahe, Francis Bacon, Newton, Pascal, Leibniz, Pasteur and finally LeVerrier, who had protested against the nomination of Darwin to become a correspondent of the Paris Academy of Sciences.[75] The article concluded with a warning to all Arabs to avoid imitating the teaching of modern times, including habits and customs which, according to the author, promoted anti-religious attitudes. Instead, he recommended looking back at 'our grandfathers' style of life which encouraged simplicity, respect and attachment to religion'.[76]

Another Jesuit who provided a major critique of Darwin's theory of evolution was Father Iskandar Turan, author of a series of articles which appeared in *al-Mashriq*, in 1921, entitled 'Al-Madhhab al-Darwini wa Asl al-Insan' (Darwin's Doctrine and the Origin of Man).[77] This work constituted one of the last major attacks on Darwinism by the Christian Arab group. Following in the footsteps of Cheikho, Turan coloured his discussion by religious convictions. Yet, in an explicit fashion, he differentiated between what he called 'radical Darwinists' and 'moderate Darwinists'. Without compromising his beliefs, Turan was prepared to accept certain evolutionary ideas, if they were God-given. Thus Turan's main target was Haeckel's notion of the origin of mankind. He felt that Haeckel's materialistic interpretation of the universe and life denied the existence of God. Unlike Cheikho, he was less critical of Darwin's ideas and considered him to be a believer.[78] Turan provided some interpretation of the Bible to accommodate the theory of evolution. He said, the term 'day' as recorded in Genesis could be interpreted to mean 'working day' which could be as long as thousands of our years. In this way, the stages of evolution could be explained.[79]

After explaining Haeckel's ideas on spontaneous generation and how Pasteur's experiment discredited them, Turan wondered how the human soul could originate from inorganic matter.[80] He also attacked Darwin's idea of natural selection. While he thought that the Bible was in agreement with Darwin's ideas on the evolution of animals and plants, Turan disagreed with its application to the creation of man. Like Cheikho, he insisted that Darwin's natural selection and its role in the creation of new species was based on false assumptions and illusions. Turan argued that natural selection was only the result of man-made selection. He explained that man's domestication of animals and plants had produced species with new characteristics. If these animals and plants were left without human care, they would lose their acquired characteristics.[81] As expected, in his conclusion, Turan asserted the role of God in the creation of all species and dismissed Darwin's view on Western scientific grounds.

A few detailed accounts of other Christian Arab reactions to Darwinism appeared in the Arabic press. Archimandrite Rufail Hawawini (d. 1915) of the Orthodox Church defended Christianity against materialism and Darwinism. He translated from Greek, from unknown sources, a series of articles under different headings. The most important one was entitled, 'Dahd Dawa al-Madiyyin min Nafs Mantiqahm' (On the Refutation of Materialism), which was published in 1888–89 in the pages of his journal, *al-Hadiya*, a weekly periodical and the official organ of the Orthodox Church.[82] As

expected, and like other religious Arabs, Hawawini was not interested in the historical and scientific aspects of Darwinism, but he
advanced opinions to distort and discredit the materialist creed of the
creation of mankind. His attack was mainly against Büchner's and
Shumayyil's ideas on the origin of life.

Hawawini, in order to make his arguments against materialism as
strong as possible, maintained that his data were drawn from the
writing of the materialists themselves.[83] He imagined two individuals,
one a materialist and the other a spiritualist, who had no doubt
whatever about God. The believer maintained that by basing himself
on the principles of materialism, he could reach the same conclusions
and beliefs as given by religion. In other words, he wanted to prove
that the theories of materialism implied a contradiction to materialist principles. He drew on the writings of those who challenged
some of the materialists' views on scientific grounds. Later in his life,
Hawawini took a new position in New York as spiritual leader of the
Orthodox Arabs residing in the United States and Canada. While in
New York, he debated Darwin's theory of evolution with another
priest, Anis Barudi. In 1906, Hawawini wrote in *al-Kalimah* (The
Word), a periodical published in New York in Arabic, that all
species were created separately and that man, no matter how diverse,
came from one root, Adam.[84] In 1908, Barudi wrote an article in
Mirat al-Gharb, (Mirror of the West) also published in New York on
Darwin's theory. In it, he considered Darwin's ideas as scientific
facts.[85] In his reply, Hawawini criticised the theory on religious
grounds, arguing that species could not be generated from other
species. He asked Barudi to be patient and wait because scientific
truth is the total sum of many truths. He added, while the Bible was
not a scientific book, still the Bible and science complemented and
did not contradict each other.[86]

CHEIKHO AND THE SECULARISTS

Cheikho's writings had no impact on the thought of Arab evolutionists. Like his religious counterparts in the West, he claimed that his
debate with Arab modernists was rooted in scientific bases, but most
of his arguments against evolution originated with scripture. While
Cheikho and other religious thinkers were not totally ignorant in
science or evolution and aimed not to attack science *per se*, Cheikho,
the Jesuit critic of Darwinism continued to use the declining anti-

Darwinian polemic that was still current in the last quarter of the nineteenth century. By doing so his rejection of Darwinism could present an appearance of being in agreement with a part of the scientific community, since it was important for his image not to reject a scientific theory on religious grounds.

Although Sarruf and Nimr argued against materialism, their writings supported the biological similarity between man and the lower species. Both frequently showed that evolution was not incompatible with any religion, including Catholicism. In other words, one could subscribe to Darwin's evolutionary thought without compromising one's religion. This clear-cut faith in God did not save the editors of *al-Muqtataf* from denunciations by Cheikho. Like other theologians, he was afraid that Darwinist thought would be a factor in destroying public beliefs, and consequently make people feel that life had no purpose. Furthermore, it seems that Cheikho frankly viewed Arab evolutionists as tending towards outright heresy.

Cheikho's debate with Arab evolutionists was not restricted to scientific issues. In his journal, Cheikho introduced Arab readers to scores of other questions on linguistic and historical matters as well. The polemical debates, regardless of their negative impact, undoubtedly provided Arab readers with the opportunity to rediscover some of their own scientific and literary heritage. While it is true that Cheikho's main concern remained religious, these intellectual battles made it possible for many young Arabs to assess and study many points of view on different aspects of Western thought. Through the scholarly work of Cheikho and his rivals, a better understanding of research methods and foreign ideas came within the reach of Arab readers.

Arab secularists had common characteristics. First they aimed to introduce to the Arab population contemporary scientific matters and methods. Second, while it is true Arab thinkers such as Shumayyil and Musa exaggerated Darwin's work, they also pointed out how external elements like religion impeded scientific development in the Arab world.

Since the group under the leadership of Cheikho could not produce scientific writing capable of competing with that of the Arab secularists, they made use of violent language and personal attack. This manner of debate was probably the only appropriate way of responding under the circumstances. Arab secularists were accused of being unscientific and atheist. Many of them, like Sarruf, Nimr and al-Yaziji, took to the offensive in order to keep their scientific journals alive. Sarruf correctly mentioned that Cheikho provided special treatment for Catholic writers.

> When somebody who is not Catholic expressed an idea that looks unsubstantiated or contrary to religious teaching, he immediately was labelled as atheist. But when it came from a Catholic, he always acted with tact, reserve and caution.[87]

In this light, it is especially significant that Cheikho steadfastly avoided even the mere mention of Shumayyil's work.

6 The Muslim Response to Darwinism

INTRODUCTION

The history of the Arab Muslim world is largely the history of reaction to a variety of political, legal, philosophical, theological and scientific ideas from the West. Muslim polemicists and theologians, like their counterparts in the West, have over the years continued to discuss the form and content of their faith in the light of scientific developments. Muslim thinkers of the Middle Ages responded to Greek sciences and philosophy in a variety of ways. Some rejected foreign thought altogether, while others acceded to it and islamicized the ideas.

In modern times, some Arabs, like the Wahhabis in Saudi Arabia, rejected everything Western as foreign and saw a return to early Islam as the only remedy for their stagnant society.[1] Others attempted to adapt Islam to the modern techniques of the West. Still others advocated the complete adoption of Western ideas in order to progress. The Muslim thinkers considered in this study supported the second and third of these points of view. Christian Arabs (whether Catholic, Protestant or Orthodox) drew heavily upon the writings of other Christian groups in the West in their efforts to challenge Western scientific ideas. Muslim Arabs were at a disadvantage, since they did not have such sources to draw upon. Christians also had central authorities, like popes and archbishops, to guide their responses, while Muslims lacked such figures. The translation of Western texts and the increased contact with the West in the nineteenth century resulted in the introduction of European scientific thought to the Arab East. Muslim scholars made use of this knowledge not only to defend Islam, but also to defend all religions.

Both Muslim and Christian scholars were alike in the sense that they had a rather illogical response to Darwinism. While the accomplishments of science at that time had increased confidence in the value of the rational understanding of the universe, the scholars concentrated their efforts to use modern science as a tool for reinforcing traditional beliefs and faith. Furthermore, at a time when Darwin's theory of evolution was becoming accepted along with other concepts of modern science, there were demands from Arab religious groups that any explanation of the origin of man which contradicted the teaching of the revealed word of God in the holy books should be refuted.

This chapter examines the conflict between Darwinism and revelation as treated by Muslim thinkers – principally Afghani, Hussein al-Jisr, Isfahani, Hasan Hussein, Ismail Mazhar and Mansuri. These thinkers were anxious about the uncertainty caused by the spread of Western scientific ideas among the Arab population. While some Muslim scholars approved of Darwinism (conditioned by the belief that all events happen by the will of Allah), others provided a better explanation of the acceptance of the evolutionary doctrine. One might add that since Muslims constituted the great majority of the Arab population, they could be viewed as more aware than the Christian minority of the impact of evolution on the main currents of Arab society.

JAMAL-AL-DIN AL-AFGHANI

The first Muslim to refute Darwin's theory was a non-Arab philosopher. He is the most well-known scholar of the group studied here. Many writers have provided analyses of his work. Some consider him a renegade, others a religious fanatic. A few even believe that atheistic tendencies are found in his writings. Here, we are only concerned with his work on Darwinism. His thoughts on the subject were presented in an essay entitled *Al-Radd ala al-Dahriyyin* (The Refutation of Materialists). Afghani wrote this study while he was in British India in 1881, it originally appeared in Persian. In 1885, Muhammad Abduh, one of Afghani's disciples, translated the text into Arabic. Jean Lucerf mentions that Abduh's translation of Afghani's *Refutation* was made in reaction to Shumayyil's ideas on evolution.[2] A. Goichon translated the same text into French in 1942 and an English translation of the *Refutation* was produced by Nikki R. Keddie in 1968. Afghani dedicated his essay to counter the spread of naturalism (*naychariyya*) which was introduced into India by Sayyid Ahmad Khan (1817–1898).[3]

Afghani's *Refutation* was part of the attempt to awaken the Muslim peoples, including the Arab world, to a new European threat. His activities took him to nearly all Muslim lands. He was partially responsible for such political events as the 1882 Urabi uprising in Egypt.[4] The main objective of Afghani's writing was political, a pan-Islamic solidarity against the West. To him, the unity of the Islamic *Umma* (community) had to be accomplished in order to meet the danger of Western powers. This could be done by accepting the fact that the strength of the West was due to knowledge and its proper application, and that the weakness of the Muslim community was due to illiteracy and ignorance: 'The Orient must learn the useful arts of Europe.'[5] The contemporary reader may not find Afghani's *Refutation* of great significance, but, as Keddie remarks, one must consider its time and place. Afghani defined naturalism as the 'Root of corruption and the source of foolishness. From it comes the ruin of the land, the perdition of man.'[6]

After reviewing the essence of Islam which, according to him, was not contrary to reason and human well being, he went on to survey the views presented by the ancient Greek thinkers and modern evolutionists on naturalism. Unlike other Muslim scholars considered in this study, Afghani probably never read any of Darwin's original work. His writing against evolution was based on confusions and misrepresentations common at that time. He presented his opposition to Darwinism in a simplistic question and answer format. He asked about the causes of variations in the trees and plants of Indian forests, all found in one soil. He asked Darwin to explain the origin of variations in fish in both Lake Aral and the Caspian Sea, for they were living in the same water and shared the same food for centuries. He sought to show that Darwin could only answer these questions by silence.

> Darwin would crumble, flabbergasted. He could not have raised his head from the sea of perplexity, had he been asked to explain the variation among the animals of different forms that live in one zone and whose existence in other zones would be difficult.[7]

As to evolution itself, Afghani provided a bizarre definition for the theory:

> One group of materialists decided that the germs of all species, especially animals, are identical, that there is no difference be-

tween them and that the species also have no essential distinction. Therefore, they said, those germs transferred from one species to another and changed from one form to another through the demands of time and place, according to need and moved by external forces.[8]

He went on to state that Darwin was the representative of the above views:

> The leader of this school is Darwin. He wrote a book stating that man descends from the monkey, and that in the course of successive centuries as a result of external impulses he changed until he reached the stage of the orangutang. From that form he rose to the earliest human degree, which was the race of cannibals and other Negroes. Then some men rose and reached a position on a higher plane than that of the Negroes, the plane of Caucasian man.[9]

According to this view, Afghani argues, 'it would be possible that after the passage of centuries a mosquito (*barghuth*)[10] could become an elephant and an elephant, by degrees, a mosquito'.[11]

Afghani cited 'Darwin's' illustration of how the continuous cutting of dogs' tails for several centuries would produce a new generation of dogs without tails, and he related this to the Semitic practices of circumcision:

> Is this wretch deaf to the fact that the Arabs and Jews for several thousand years have practiced circumcision, and despite this until now not one of them has been born circumcised?[12]

Afghani went on to attack materialists (*Naycheris*) on the basis that matter, force and intelligence alone could not produce such a perfect order of things in the universe. His attack came in a series of questions, like:

> How did these separate, scattered particles become aware of each other's aims and by what instrument of explanation did they explain their affairs? In what parliament and senate did they confer in order to form these elegant and wonderful beings?[13]

These were the kinds of questions that Afghani provoked among Arab readers. They were not easily solvable and for this reason, perhaps, he had not hesitated to attack materialism rather severely. Although he was Persian, his influence was especially marked in the Arab world.

Afghani's attack on materialism resembles those of Nimr and Sarruf who refuted materialism on the ground that it never took into account the question of soul as a divine power in the process of creation.[14] While he admired Shumayyil's courageous stand in favour of Darwinism and modern philosophy, he accused him of being a blind imitator of Western scientists.[15] Yet, he never failed to recognize the importance of modern scientific thought and its impact on Islam. In fact, he rejected both pure traditional belief and the blind adoption of Western ideas.

As mentioned earlier, Arab religious writers such as Cheikho often referred favourably to Afghani as well as to other religious writers whose work supported the role of God in the process of creation. Arab secularists such as Farah Antun (1874–1922), a Christian from Syria, did not attach much importance to Afghani's ideas.[16] While in New York, Antun published a series of articles on both Afghani and Abduh. Ismail Mazhar, a Muslim Egyptian, also discredited Afghani's *Refutation* as we will see later in this chapter.

Here we are mainly concerned with Antun's critique of Afghani's *Refutation*.[17] Antun started his critique by asking if Afghani had any philosophy, in the sense of modern Western philosophers. In this respect, Antun stated that Afghani was only a religious reformer. Antun pointed out that although Afghani's meagre ideas gained ground in the Muslim world due to the strong position of his disciples, such as Abduh, he only published one essay, the *Refutation*. And for this reason when *al-Muqtataf* was asked to write about Afghani's work, the editor answered that he did not know anything about his ideas. Sarruf and Nimr, both Christian secularists, did not even mention Afghani's ideas on Darwinism.[18]

Antun found Afghani's religious scheme unworkable. He dismissed the notion that on the basis of a unified vision based on the Islamic faith, the Islamic world could reach the level of development of Western nations, which adopted the essence of natural sciences. By concentrating on Islamic faith rather than on science, Antun asserted, two unfortunate consequences would ensue. First, the people would become more dependent on religious beliefs and not adopt the natural sciences. Second, as a result of actual differences of upbringing among the population, people would find themselves completely occupied with religious dogmas – even sacrifice their lives for it – while religious and business leaders exploited the poor and acquired wealth, amassing political, religious and social power.[19] While he did not oppose the combination of power and religion to create an important civilization, as in the case of the ancient Islamic world, Antun rejected the priority given to the individual's religious education before his mental and physical faculties could be built up. The motives behind Afghani's *Refutation*, Antun said, were mainly political ambition. It was his way to attain leadership in Islamic circles. Antun, in his conclusion, compared Afghani's simplistic interpretations of Darwinism and religion with those of a primary school boy.[20]

Commenting on Afghani's method of building the Eastern *Nahdah* (awakening) on honesty, trust, the belief in God and eternity, and the individuals belief in his religion, Antun insisted:

> The Hindus in India, whose religion was considered by Afghani as inferior to Islam and whose social development was the same as the Muslims 26 years ago [the time when Afghani wrote his *Refutation*], have now by-passed their Muslim counterparts.[21]

Antun alluded to the development of science and social thought among Hindus.

During Afghani's short stay in France, he took issue with Ernest Renan on science and Islam, publishing in the pages of the *Journal des débats* of 18 May 1883. His letter was written in reply to Renan's talk on Islam and science, delivered at the Sorbonne on 29 March 1883. Renan's main arguments were that the Islamic religion was the reason for Arab backwardness and what had been called Arab science was only written in Arabic by non-Arab thinkers.[22] In this talk, Renan was clearly antagonistic to Arabs and Islam. He claimed that Islam hindered the progress of science and free thought when it was strong and allowed advancement only when it was weak.

After praising Renan's views, Afghani asserted that not only Islam, but all religions, 'in their origin were not guided by pure reason'.[23] He wrote:

> One cannot deny that it is by this religious education, whether it be Muslim, Christian or pagan, that all nations have emerged from barbarism and marched toward a more advanced civilization.[24]

While Afghani agreed with Renan on the attempt of Islam to

suppress the development of science, he added that Christian churches, especially the Catholic one, still act in the same manner. Yet Afghani was of the opinion that all religious teachings were instruments in liberating humanity from ignorance and barbarism. Afghani also mentioned that Christians had succeeded first in their battle against religious dogma, because Christianity was the older religion, preceding Islam. The Muslim world could one day achieve the same success as Western society.[25] Afghani argued that the Arab accomplishment in science and philosophy equalled those of other nations. Commenting on non-Arab contributions to science he stated:

As for Ibn-Bajja, Ibn Rushd (Averroes), and Ibn Tufayl, one cannot say that they are not just as Arab as al-Kindi because they were not born in Arabia, especially if one is willing to consider that human races are only distinguished by their languages and that if this distinction should disappear, nations would not take long to forget their diverse origins. And if all Europeans belong to the same stock, one can with justice claim that the Harranians and the Syrians, who are Semites, belong to the great Arab Family.[26]

As to the question of Arab civilization, which after its glory in science suddenly became stagnant, Afghani admitted that 'the responsibility of the Muslim religion appears to stifle the sciences completely'.[27] In his confusion, Afghani said that the conflict between science and religion would never end.

Later in his life, Afghani seemed to provide a better explanation of Darwin's ideas. His views differed in degree only, and not in kind, from that of *The Refutation*. Muhammad al-Makhzumi, the editor of *Khatirat al-Afghani* (The Thought of Afghani), provided a review of Afghani's ideas on evolution.[28] In a section entitled 'Afghani's Opinion of the Doctrine of Evolution and Progress', Afghani was asked what Abu al-Ala al-Maarri, an ancient Arab philosopher, meant when he wrote a poem in which one of its verses explained that 'animals were generated from inorganic matter'.[29] Afghani's reply was that al-Maarri meant evolution and progress as other Arab philosophers before him had explained how mud could transform to plant and plant into animal. In this respect, while Afghani accepted evolution, he added, 'If the doctrine of evolution is based on these premises, then the Arab scientists preceded Darwin.'[30]

So, convinced about the comprehensive writings on ancient Arab philosophers, Afghani claimed that the works found in the ancient

Arab libraries of Baghdad, Al-Andalus (Spain), and Al-Qayrawan, including Arab translations and writings on philosophy and natural sciences, were equivalent – if not superior – to all sciences brought from the modern West.[31] Natural selection was attributed to pre-Islamic and Islamic culture. He claimed that Arabs, in their search for better horses and wives, had long applied this concept. While Afghani, later in his life, softened his stand on Darwin by separating him from the materialists Spencer, Büchner and Shumayyil, he insisted on the special creation of man. Still confused about Darwin's scientific achievement in explaining evolution, he considered classical Arab poets and philosophers the inventors of this idea.

Afghani provided a rallying point for those who rejected Darwin's universe. He provided a simplistic refutation of Darwinism based on traditional Arab values. He substituted for Darwin's scientific evidence on natural selection by claiming that Arabs had regularly applied this principle. Denying the evolutionary process, Afghani held that life did not develop at random and that there was a plan in the creation of species.

HUSSEIN AL-JISR

Al-Jisr was born in Tripoli, Lebanon, and belonged to the Muslim Shiite sect. Many educated Arabs studied under his guidance, such as Rashid Rida, the editor of the religious journal *Al-Manar*. He wrote more than 25 books on different aspects of Muslim religion. The most important of these was *Al-Risala al-Hamidiyya fi Haqiqat al-Diana al-Islamiyya wa-Haqiqat al-Sharia al-Muhamadiyya* (A Hamedian Essay on the Truthfulness of Islamic Religion and the Truthfulness of Islamic Canon Law). It was published in Beirut in 1887 and exceeded 400 pages. This book won a prize from Sultan Abd al-Hamid, al-Jisr's patron.

In the introduction, al-Jisr wrote that he was very impressed with a certain Arab journal's translation of the English Bishop Isaac Taylor's writings on how to bring harmony between Christianity and Islam. He observed that some British Orientalists wanted to build a mosque and publish an Arab paper to investigate the truth about Islam. These events stimulated the author to write a book on the reality of Islam and to refute the materialist-naturalist principles that claimed that there was no creator of the universe.

His discussions of the concepts of materialism and Darwin were meticulous and clear. The argument was in the form of a dialogue between a materialist and an Islamic thinker. The drift of the discussions was religious and philosophical, emphasizing that the essence of Islam is a belief in God and that materialism is based on guesswork and unfounded hypotheses. Al-Jisr's discussion is accurate and impressive. Unlike Afghani, he did not confuse the proposition that man and ape came from the same origin. Al-Jisr did not differentiate, at this stage, between Darwin's ideas and materialist thought, nor between materialists and naturalists. Unlike other Arabs, he did not even mention the names of Darwin or Shumayyil. His main concern was to define Islamic law against atheism and not to attack personalities. Al-Jisr took every effort to refute the materialists' claims and restore confidence in God as the sole creator of this universe.[32]

Convinced of Islamic excellence and past brilliance, he called upon the materialists to adopt Islam and be saved from their agony and despair of disbelief. His emphasis upon the positive qualities of Islam led him to accept almost all evolutionary processes and even materialistic ideas. This acceptance was due to his conviction that the Quran contained all scientific knowledge.

In al-Jisr's view, materialism was unable to provide explanations of all natural phenomena. He wrote, 'There are numerous laws in this materialistic world which we do not know yet and scientists are discovering new laws every day.'[33] He elaborated on this point to demonstrate the existence of God. Scientists had 'discouraged us from believing that there are certain facts beyond this material world'.[34] He considered the example of electricity: 'We could not see it with our eyes, yet we feel its results in our daily life.'[35] He continued with a proposition that would have been entirely acceptable to Western scientists:

Not to believe in the existence of a thing unless we comprehend it by our senses, is not acceptable in all circumstances; we may deviate from this position. We believe in the ether without depending on our senses; what requires its acceptance is our need to know the truth about light.[36]

Al-Jisr explained how materialism accounted for the origin of the universe and the nature of matter, mass, and its forces in creating the roots of living organisms and inert matter. He articulated the process of the growth of populations among animals and plants. He attributed this process to four natural laws: first, variation in individual species, where every individual does not exactly resemble its fore-bears; second, variations carried from parents to off-spring, which produced strong and weak organisms, relative to environmental conditions; third, the struggle for survival among individuals, evident when the weak perished; finally, nature selected the strongest and the fittest to survive. According to these laws, the author continued:

Man, himself, is considered not more than an animal; like other animals, he progressed and developed through natural process to reach his present stage. Man's resemblance to ape did not prevent him and the ape from coming from the same origin.[37] . . . Man's mind and intellect is part of the many forms of the action and rèaction of his matter and its movable components. Since the origin of matter and motion is without mind and intellect, man's mind does not differ essentially from the mind of other animals, except in quantity.[38]

Al-Jisr's immediate reaction to materialism was its acceptance, provided the proponents of the ideas agreed with the notion that 'natural phenomena were explainable by the power of God, who is able to make them.'[39] He provided the example of a clock that was built to extremely accurate measurements. 'Obviously this clock could not exist without a maker.'[40] He used another technical example:

Suppose somebody prepared parts of a steam engine and later we found the engine assembled and in full operation. Is it more acceptable to our reason to say that the parts were assembled by their maker, or that the parts, with time, assembled and become operational by themselves?[41]

God, in his view was the great mechanic.

In his effort to sharpen the distinction between people of faith and materialists, al-Jisr drew on certain natural phenomena that could not be explained by science. He asked about why, in a magnetic field, the force of attraction was weaker in the middle than in the extremities.[42] He also asked the naturalists to explain how motion was transformed to electric power, the latter changed to heat, and heat to light. He answered his own questions. Recognition of God's wisdom and purpose was crucial to understanding these phenomena. There was no way that scientists could know the causes of natural phenomena simply by observation and experiment.[43] Al-Jisr did not realize that the same reasoning could be applied to divine laws.

The most convincing and heavily documented section of al-Jisr's work dealt with the interpretation of *Shariah* to suit the new scientific thought. The author insisted that the true nature of Islam is to seek progress. It rejects the attempt of apologists to interpret the Quran in a way contrary to its original meaning. Because nothing in the Quran opposed empirical evidence, al-Jisr argued that when new evidence appeared to contradict the literal meaning of some verses of the Quran, *tawil* (interpretation) of these verses must be used to suit modern realities.[44] Drawing on al-Razi, the famous ancient Arab commentator, al-Jisr added that if there were no absolute empirical evidence to contradict the Quran, one should refrain from *tawil* and keep silent.

Turning to Darwin's theory, al-Jisr made every effort to show how Quranic verses, if interpreted in the proper manner, could provide similar explanation of the theory of evolution. To this end he quoted the following verses:

> 'We made every living thing from water. Will they not then believe?' XXI:30; in another place the Quran says: 'Allah hath created every animal from water,' XXIV:45; 'and that He createth the two spouses, the male and the female from a drop (of seed) when it is poured forth' LIII:45 and 46; 'verily We created man from a product of wet earth; then placed him as a drop (of seed) in a safe lodging; then fashioned We the drop a clot, then fashioned We the clot a little lump, then fashioned We the little lump bones, then clothed the bones with flesh, and then produced it as another creation.' XXIII:12–14.[45]

Al-Jisr argued that the first two verses provided that life first originated in water and agreed with the theory of evolution and creation.[46] The other verses, he added, appeared to denote special creation for every species but, in fact, 'There is no further evidence in the Quran to suggest whether all species, each of which exists by the grace of God, were created all at once or gradually.'[47] Here, it is clear that al-Jisr accepted the process of evolutionary development and suggested that God was able to create species suddenly or gradually. He called for the retention of traditional religious values until further work justified additional expansion of the realm of science. He urged Muslims to believe the Quran on creation until further empirical evidence supported the theory of evolution. Al-Jisr drew on al-Razi's interpretation of the origin of man. He said that water and mud lay at the origin of life. After quoting verses from the Quran, he pointed out that God created life from lifeless matter.

Al-Jisr seriously attempted to reconcile Islam with modern science, especially Darwin's work. He was ready to accept modern realities which would not contradict Islamic values. In a school that he founded in his native village, Al-Jisr provided for teaching, among other subjects, mathematics and natural science.[48] He explained, with the help of *tawil*, that Islamic conceptions of evolution and science correspond closely to modern facts. Although al-Jisr was able to explain the role of natural selection and survival of the fittest as mechanisms of variations leading to the emergence of new species, he was reluctant to accept them before conclusive intellectual evidence (*dalil aqli qati*) established their validity. When that happened, he was willing to interpret the Quran to accommodate the new evidence.

ABU AL-MAJID MUHAMMAD RIDA AL-ISFAHANI

Isfahani, a prominent Shiite theologian from Karbula, Iraq, wrote a book of two parts entitled *Naqd Falsafat Darwin* (Critique of Darwin's Philosophy), which appeared in 1914 and reflected the Muslim Shiite accommodation to Western ideas in general and to Darwin's evolutionary thought in particular.[49] Isfahani wrote the book to attack *al-Muattila* (Those Who Would Deny God His Attributes) and bigoted divines. He wanted to defend not only Islam, but all religions, against atheist evidence contradicting beliefs in God. In a special message to believers, he added:

> My book was to defend absolute religion, as opposed to mere non-religion, and at the same time not to promote one religion above others. Therefore, you see me defending religions that I did not belong to and doctrines I do not subscribe to because the transmission of a distorted version of any religion by *al-Muattila* would lead to the distortion of all religions.[50]

Unlike Shumayyil, Musa and Cheikho, Isfahani claimed that he adopted the scientific method of inquiry in his work on Darwinism. As a religious leader he, perhaps, did not want to be viewed as a dogmatic thinker. Isfahani insisted that he would never side with any theory nor accept it as an absolute certainty. He urged his readers not to side with his ideas nor repeat them without verifying the evidence.[51] He used simple terms and colloquial terminology. His writings usually attracted a wide audience of many faiths and, to keep his readership, he urged people to avoid fanaticism and read his work without prejudgement and bias.[52] In general, Isfahani welcomed criticism. This inclination, he added, was in accordance with the principles of *al-Kitab* (another name for the Quran), which urged independent thinking. But what Isfahani did not mention was his lack of reference material. He justified the lack on the bases of economy and brevity. He provided original sources, though, on request.

Isfahani's study was divided into two parts: the first criticized Darwin's doctrine from the religious and the scientific viewpoint; the second provided the evidence and justification for the criticism. Before starting his discussion, he asserted that his writings on Darwin's ideas did not reflect his own beliefs, since they applied natural laws to religious facts.[53] This apologetic style of writing reflected the prevailing mood against Darwin's views on the origin of man.

Isfahani opened his book with the Muslim motto, 'in the name of God, the merciful, the compassionate'. He mentioned the role played by Islam and its scientific achievements which brought Arabs from the *jahiliyya* (time of ignorance) to the rational age. Isfahani explained how Westerners, who took their sciences from the Islamic world, advanced to a point where Muslims had no choice but to borrow from them. Arabs borrowed not only what suited their progress but also some ideas which were harmful and unfit for the needs of Muslims. In other words, he condemned the indiscriminate translation into Arabic of Western writings. Isfahani wanted to see Muslims studying science in Arabic.

Isfahani's views on evolution and religion

Unlike Shumayyil and Musa, Isfahani advocated that man's knowledge of his religious duties and ancient science had to precede his involvement with modern Western thought. By following this path the individual would broaden his horizon and be able to identify scientific facts.[54]

Isfahani's insistence that religious teachings preceded the learning of modern science may be attributed to his dissatisfaction with some of his contemporaries, Shumayyil, for example, whom he accused of imitating Western thought. Isfahani remarked that 'an individual who is free in his thought, who advanced an opinion (*ijtihad*) but erred in judgement, is better than an imitator who is right'.[55]

In his view, the doctrine of evolution was not an atheistic principle because it did not deny the existence of the Creator; the materialist interpretation of the doctrine, however, led to atheism. On the question of whether all species had special creation or were founded originally by mere chance, Isfahani wrote that nothing could be found in the *Kitab* (Quran) or *sunna* (tradition) to deny either. He added, 'what difference would it make if the fathers of camels were camels, or frogs sing in the water, or the grandfather of an elephant was elephant, or a bird flies in the air, since the evidence of creation in all cases is obvious – God's work'.[56]

He presented a reasonably complete summary of the opinions advanced by evolutionists who believed in God. He aimed at discussing the views of divine evolutionists and later the *muattila*, the materialists, without necessarily sharing their beliefs. In other words, his object was to comment upon and refute those who did not adequately support their position.

Evolutionists whom he labelled as believers in God were Lamarck, Wallace, Huxley, Spencer and Darwin. Isfahani attributed to Lamarck alone the theory of creation as well as the success of Darwin's doctrine without any attempt to explain the differences between the two evolutionary approaches. Unlike Cheikho, who considered Lamarck an atheist, Isfahani defended Lamarck on the ground that he held the same views as believers, except on the question of how creation occurred. Isfahani had nothing new to add to Wallace's religious conviction except to admire his remarks on the necessity of heavenly forces to guide the evolutionary process of species.[57]

Huxley, who coined the term 'agnostic' (*al-Laadri*), was defended by Isfahani. Huxley's attitude, according to Isfahani, implied unspoken acceptance of God's wisdom. Most importantly, Isfahani accepted Huxley's differentiation between science as a rational activity and religion as a separate sphere of interest.[58] In this respect, Isfahani was almost ready to divide science from religion. Isfahani found Spencer's reference to the unknown forces of nature 'as a sign of being not far from monotheism'. Again, Isfahani differed from Cheikho who considered Spencer an unbeliever. Darwin, the last evolutionist discussed by Isfahani, was credited for his religious commitment. Isfahani like most other contemporary Arabs, emphasized the religious commitment of evolutionists because he believed that religions, as revealed through holy books, are the main source of present and future knowledge.

Isfahani insisted that scientific theories change according to the opinions of those who initiated them. Religion was opposed to this confusion. The inadequacy of theories to account once and for all for natural phenomena led Isfahani to believe that religion could not contradict well-established scientific truths. On the contrary, scientific truths did not oppose religion. He added that any new scientific discovery only supported the hidden facts of the true religion, and 'when the naturalists and the materialists failed in their scientific efforts, the role of religion became quite clear'.[59] He advanced the view that the literal translation of a religioius text like *al-Wahi* (revelation) on the creation of man could not be applied to scientific findings. One could see, in the pages of Genesis and the Quran, many metaphors such as 'God moulded Adam from soil and blew life into Adam's nose'. These metaphors did not mean that God actually performed the deed, as such.[60] Religious metaphor was really contrary to the truth of creation. The truth was only reached by scientific investigation. For example, Isfahani urged Muslims not to accept the evidence provided by some writers on the animal origin of man because these writers were unable to explain the origin of all species.[61] He used science in his own cause.

Another example of Isfahani's approach in his judgement that the evolutionists were not alone in their belief that man had arisen from a lower species. The savage tribes, before them, also chose to belong to animal species, like deer and frogs. He referred to a legend where a tribe claimed that an ape was their ancestor. The tribe's ape married a devil. The off-spring, after eating wheat provided by the ape, saw their tails become shorter and their hair fall out. They spoke, and were transformed into humans.[62] He mentioned this story to show how man was debased not only by savage tribes but also by civilized philosophers.

To deal with Darwin's comparative anatomy between man and mammals, Isfahani discussed the work of ancient Arab scholars on the similarity between man and ape. Wishing to establish a considerable degree of physical autonomy for man, the author began by citing *Kitab al-Tawhid* by al-Iman Jaafar Bin Muhammad al-Sadiq, which provided a comparative study of the physical and physiological resemblance between man and monkey. In it, al-Imam asserted that nothing could prevent the monkey from catching up with humans if he possessed a mind and the ability to speak as man.[63] Isfahani then mentioned another ancient Muslim scholar, al-Dumiri, who also explained not only the physical and structural similarity between man and ape, but also mentioned the tendency of the ape to comprehend, act, laugh, marry and learn like humans. After quoting Ikhwan al-Safa's messages, another ancient Arab work which provided comprehensive discussion of this similarity, Isfahani asserted that no matter how Darwin exaggerated the moral and physical similarities between man and ape, he would never provide more coverage on this subject than Ikhwan al-Safa had provided.[64] Isfahani emphasized that a mere mention of the resemblance between man and ape was not enough to explain the transformation of one to the other. Mere affinity of characteristics would imply that humans could evolve backward to the ape by the forces of nature, Isfahani added, a process that in itself did not contradict Islam.

In this respect, Isfahani echoed the writing of Richard Owen, I. I. Mechnikov and others on the comparative study of animal anatomy. Isfahani asserted that comparative anatomy only indicated the similarity between man and ape and left other aspects of dissimilarities between them undiscussed.[65] He added that although evolutionists, such as Richard Owen, recognized the deep mental gap between man and upper ape, the fact remained that the human being could be distinguished as human by his mental ability to solve scientific questions rather than by his organic resemblance.[66] Isfahani mentioned that 'man is human by reason of his soul; it is not his physical structuring which makes him a human'.[67] Like Cheikho, he called for a clear-cut distinction between the human mind and animal instinct.[68]

In his attempt to correct misconceptions about Darwin's evolution, Isfahani maintained that some of Darwin's enemies tried to misinterpret his views on the origin of man. They wrote that the ape is the origin of man, rather than that 'man, ape, horse and other living organisms came from one origin'.[69] By this, he meant that in the West, as in the East, there were certain elements who tried to promote false ideas about Darwin's theory of evolution. Thus, after crediting Western readers for their knowledge of such misconceptions, Isfahani added that 'the West is the brother of the East, and all people are the off-spring of one father and mother'.[70]

Isfahani's next point of contention with Darwin was on embryological similarities between man and other animals. Isfahani disputed the embryological argument stipulating that the individual, during the process of his embryonic development, followed the pattern of growth common to his own species or repeated the stages in the growth of his ancestors: ontogeny, for Isfahani, did not recapitulate phylogeny. After reading other biological texts on the same subject, including the work of Yuhana Wortabat, an Arab Christian who taught medicine at the SPC, he remained firm: 'Even if the embryological arguments were correct, still one finds two individual species of the same level of evolutionary development producing fetuses of different forms.'[71] He took the example of frogs which live in the United States, as contrasted with frogs living elsewhere in the world. He noted that the former produce embryos different from the latter.[72] To make his argument more convincing, Isfahani referred to an article published in an unknown Arabic journal by a Christian Arab leader, the Patriarch of Aleppo, F. Jianini, in 1908, entitled 'Al-Din wa al-Ilmaniya' (Religion and Scientism). In it, Jianini discussed how Haeckel falsified his data on the form of embryos to support his materialistic assumptions. Jianini also quoted Loring C. Brace's experiments to counter Haeckel's fraud in science. After describing this incident, Isfahani asserted that 'without men of religion and the effort of one of their societies, like the Kepler League [a quasi-religious association established to combat the Monist League, an atheist society created by Haeckel], fraud would remain part of the body of modern science.'[73]

Isfahani also examined Darwin's theory on the existence of nonfunctional organs in higher animals. Isfahani mentioned that these organs were exceptional. According to him, there were certain animals that, while still in the fetus stage, acquired anomalies. These anomalies in the creation of animals could not be justified by the principle of atavism.[74] Unconvinced about Darwin's discussion on the nature of non-functional organs, he added:

Can we assume that because the function of the unused organs is unknown to us, they are non-functional? By so doing, we close the door to scientific investigations of the nature of these organs. Darwin himself was not sure of the function of the organs.[75]

Isfahani proposed that research on non-functional organs not be abandoned.

He went on to discuss the hermaphroditic condition as a prerequisite for evolution. This condition, as explained by the evolutionists, contradicted not only religious teachings but also their own ideas. He added:

The evolutionists provided that man evolved from higher animals, which acquired their breasts after passing through a hermaphroditic stage. This refutes another proposition provided by the same evolutionists, to the effect that man evolved from animals where the separation between feminine and masculine took place a long time ago.[76]

In a footnote, Isfahani wondered 'why the shameful hermaphroditic condition remained apparent in man and not in lower species like hoofed animals?'

Isfahani's scientific discussion of Darwinism was philosophical and religious, rather than scientific. His merit is that he insisted, in his methodology, on following an objective view on Darwin's theory. He concentrated his attack on Büchner, the atheist, who placed natural selection instead of God in the process of creation. It is to be supposed that Isfahani's work emerged from his devotion to traditional ideas. He said that the struggle for existence, which prevented each species from overpopulating the earth and acted as an agent to keep equilibrium in nature, could not be applied to all natural events. Environmental catastrophes, like volcanoes, floods or very high or very low temperature lay outside the working of this principle.[77]

He also questioned the concept of a struggle for existence on the ground that man, the master of the kingdoms of plants and animals, kills animals and destroys trees, not because they compete with him but for his own well-being. The same applies, he added, to animals, which compete with others in a variety of ways. He provided the example of fights between lions and the rhinos, where lions fear the herbivores but not *vice-versa*. Such competition, he added, could not lend support to the struggle among species at the same level of development.[78]

Isfahani also questioned the very assumption that the most successful individual in the struggle for life is the one with certain physical or mental characteristics. He underlined the fact that some individuals with sound mental power or physical strength killed themselves, and others despite their weaknesses remained alive. To support his views, he referred in a footnote to an ancient Arab poet who wrote: 'Generosity leads to poverty, and courage leads to death.'[79] This verse could be applied to courageous men and animals who fought until their death. As to the struggle among plants, Isfahani claimed that there are certain plants that without human care, could not compete with other plants of the same kind.

Isfahani's next difference with Darwin was on the extent to which the struggle for survival causes transformation among living organisms and thus leads to evolution. He made his dissent clear by pointing out that certain characteristics of living individuals may be selected during the struggle between the weak and the strong. The weak individual could also produce a new generation with modified and improved organs without necessarily endangering the transformation and modification of the strong.[80] Thus, for Isfahani, the struggle for existence not only constitutes a factor in the process of evolution, but also serves as an element in restoring the balance of nature. Isfahani noted that the example of giraffes supported his argument: the death of giraffes with short necks cannot be the cause of the length of the necks of members of the species as a whole.

On the question of variation in species, Isfahani, though accepting the general norms of transmutation, insisted that every living organism produces a living one similar to it; the off-spring has the essential characteristics of its parents. And that is why, he added, 'the horse does not produce a dog or a cat, but rather an animal resembling him'.[81] The fixity of species was due to heavenly wisdom.

Isfahani's next question was on the sexual selection. He agreed with Darwin's ideas that selection of this kind was practised among savage tribes where the strongest and bravest men married beautiful women. But he, like Afghani, disagreed with Darwin on sexual selection among plants and animals. Isfahani asked, 'how can one explain the beauty among plant variation and how do animals select the most beautiful of their kind as a mate?' The selection, he continued, could not be based on blind natural forces and suggested instead a new selection based on divine authority. He called it 'al-tahsin al-Ilahi' (divine amelioration) instead of natural selection.[82]

In underlining the evolutionists' inability to explain the multiplication of certain species' characteristics, Isfahani, correctly discussed Lamarck's ideas on the cause of evolution and examined Schopenhauer's and Samuel Butler's ideas on the necessity for the creation of organs in species. His objection to the latter came in the form of an example. He wrote 'if necessity caused the creation of horns for an ox, who required them to fight, why was the same necessity not applied to man, who always desired to have wings to fly to a tryst with his beloved?'[83] He also objected to Lamarck's ideas by injecting his argument on inverse evolution. Isfahani provided the example of the black bear, which was much stronger centuries ago and under the impact of certain environmental changes had regressed to his present weakness.[84] Again, it should be noted that Isfahani was not so much denying the operation of natural selection in the emergence of new species, as attempting to show that God's wisdom had a primary role in the process of speciation.

In his reading of Shumayyil's translation of Büchner's commentary on Darwin, Isfahani found that Büchner misread Darwin's ideas on the origin of species because Büchner thought that Darwin did not have the courage to say that all living matter came from one origin. It was not lack of courage, Isfahani thought, but the circumstance that Darwin relied on evidence and proven facts.[85] In his attack against those who believe only in the natural forces, like Büchner and perhaps Shumayyil (Isfahani referred, explicitly to his book and without mentioning his name), Isfahani, like Cheikho, embarked on a detailed account of scientists who had combined religious convictions and scientific work. Among others, he mentioned Newton, Harvey and Pasteur. The last, according to Isfahani, succeeded in destroying the false claim of the materialists on spontaneous generation.[86] He also mentioned that this concept was known to ancient Arab thinkers, like Ibn Sina whose work on spontaneous generation, though lacking experimental support, provided a good introduction to the subject.

The author concluded his first book by treating the idea of progress (*taqaddum*), a concept echoed by many Arab thinkers. Following Spencer, Isfahani recognized the importance of progress, which, he wrote, led to perfection among living things.[87] Yet he questioned the meaning given to perfection by Spencer. According to Spencer, Isfahani reported, progress leads to the disappearance of redundant organs. If this were true, Isfahani felt, man could end up with one eye, one leg and one hand. Isfahani also referred to Joseph Le Conte's idea that an increase in the number of similar organs led to degradation while a decrease resulted in strength, and to Büchner's thought that the specialization of organs provided an index of evolutionary advancement. Isfahani noted that small animals that had no need for lungs did not necessarily belong to lower species. If one organ could perform many functions at the same time, then there is no need for other organs to share the same function. Like Cheikho and Afghani, Isfahani affirmed that the structural unity of living organisms was the result of heavenly wisdom and not the consequence of blind chance in nature.[88] Isfahani, while accepting Darwin's ideas on variations in species, required the identification of first causes.

Since the process of evolution required only a minute difference between species, Isfahani asked, why did some evolutionists create a great divide to separate man from animal; sometimes they upgraded animal and debased man and sometimes the reverse, according to their vision of animal intelligence. Like Cheikho, Isfahani asserted that what came from animals was caused by forces that differed from those of man. In other words, he pointed out that while animals depend on their instinct to meet their needs, humans depend on their mind.[89]

Isfahani concluded the first part of his book by labelling the materialists' interpretation of natural laws as mere guesswork while at the same time defending some of Darwin's ideas on evolution. While his refutation of some aspects of natural selection and survival of the fittest was sound, he insisted on the role of God in the systematic structure of species. He led his readers to believe that the multiple divergence and distribution of species could be accounted for only by the will of God and that scientific discoveries were entrusted in nature by the Creator's purpose. Isfahani tried to affirm that all knowledge and scientific discoveries could be explained through one medium – the word of God.

In the second part of Isfahani's work the drift of argument was religious.[90] After having refuted the atheists, he furnished evidence of God's purpose in creating an orderly universe. He repeated his earlier theme that believers recognized and accepted every newly discovered natural law on the condition that the law conforms to the criterion of evidence. Religion would not be harmed by accepting scientific results, he felt. Believers would even be confirmed in their convictions by following the latest scientific discoveries.[91]

Isfahani's discussion was in the form of a dialogue between an atheist and a believer who travelled by ship to attend a fair (*maarad*) in New York. His main concern was to refute the materialistic view of Büchner and Shumayyil. The initial stage of dialogue ended with the success of the believer in finding a contradiction in the atheist's argument. The believer declared that although the materialist advocated the infinity of matter without knowing the reasons for it, he admitted that this ignorance could not be explained in terms of science, but is rather a matter of faith. To the believer, this faith was precisely the faith of those who believe in the wisdom of God.[92] Faith in the eternity of matter would appear to the believer as a conviction similar to the belief in God who created all things according to his comprehensive knowledge. The materialist and the believer, then, were equal in their appeal to metaphysics. The believer emphasized:

> There is no distinction between seeing the actual thing itself or feeling its results, because if one believed, for example, in the existence of electricity without being able to smell it and touch it, why then not believe in the existence of God as the Creator of the universe, even though He is invisible to us.[93]

In his attack on materialistic ideas, Isfahani mentioned that Büchner misunderstood Aristotle on the matter. Isfahani, after referring to some of Plato's work, affirmed that although Aristotle did not deny the special creation of matter he credited God's with the power to organise its motion.[94] As expected, towards the end of the conversation between the atheist and the believer, the latter seemed to persuade the former of his rational arguments. The atheist, therefore, thanked the believer who helped him to see 'the light of trust' and, as such, rejected materialist guesswork.[95]

Isfahani also took aim at Shumayyil's rejection of religion. Relying mostly on ethical judgement and on ancient Arab scientific accomplishments under Islamic rule, Isfahani rejected Shumayyil's assertion that nations progressed only when religion was weak, and *vice-versa*.[96] He provided the examples of the Hebrew and Arab nations who progressed only after adopting religion.[97] While Shumayyil's opposition was not against religion *per se*, he opposed the practice of religious leaders in using religion for political and private benefits. This attack on religious leaders incited Isfahani to extend his criticism not only to Shumayyil but also to the entire 'infidel class of Darwinians'. Isfahani claimed that Shumayyil and Musa ignored the positive effects of religion, which helped to preserve rather than shed human blood. He reminded both authors to look at the darker side of the idea of superman, which extolled killing the weak, the sick and the unfit, as well as permitting adultery and polyandry.[98]

Commenting on Shumayyil's discussion of how religion restricted freedom of thought, Isfahani seemed to contradict himself. As we have already seen, Isfahani insisted on adopting religion before studying science, and he never accepted materialism as a scientific principle. Yet, he claimed:

> Religion did not compete with science because the former differs

from the latter and it is counterproductive on the part of religion to
restrict thought. After all, religion was not a geometry book which
teaches that every two angles in a triangle total more than 180
degrees.[99]

As for Shumayyil's emphasis on the persistence of natural science as
opposed to literary works, Isfahani provided an interesting remark
similar to those furnished by today's anti-technology movement. He
wrote 'did not the natural sciences which he [Shumayyil] praised,
now become tools in the hands of leaders and the strong to expand
and to destroy people?'[100] He also referred to the French Revolution,
which was presumably based on scientific doctrines, as an atheist
movement that killed more than ten thousand people. The success of
the French Revolution was due, he felt, to the religious revolution of
Martin Luther.

Isfahani's work indicates that the discussion on Darwin's theory
was not confined to Cairo and Beirut, the nineteenth-century centres
of Arab scientific activities. Judged by Isfahani's comprehensive
coverage of Darwinism, one can assume interest in the subject on the
part of the Iraqi Shiite population. Furthermore, Isfahani's effort in
providing a broad popularisation of Darwinism not only to the
educated elite but also to the public at large can be interpreted as a
regional diffusion of Darwinian thought among Arab and Iranian
Shiites. The context for the reception of Isfahani's writings includes
the community of educated Shiite Iranians who contributed articles
to an Arab periodical *al-Irfan*, whose editor was a Shiite Lebanese
from Tripoli. Literate Shiites, who constituted the majority among
the Muslim population of Iran, Iraq and Lebanon, could well have
been familiar with Darwinism through this and other vehicles.

One cannot, of course, disregard the central importance given to
religion by Isfahani. Religous ethos and values were used at many
turns in his arguments. Isfahani's insistence that religions are not
contrary to science but follow what science teaches, by no means
resulted in a victory for rational thought. It only provided evidence
for the fundamental incommensurability of science and religion.
Despite Isfahani's philosophical and religious criticism of certain
aspects of Darwinism, his work is without doubt a milestone in the
dissemination of Western scientific ideas among the Arab and Muslim readers in the East.

Isfahani's diffusion of Western scientific ideas to the Arab Islamic
world was almost without confusion. To Isfahani, some of Darwin's

ideas were unsubstantiated and open to scientific investigation. Yet he regarded provisional scientific formulations as proof of facts hidden in the word of God. Even if these unsettled ideas proved to be correct, Isfahani considered them as supporting religion. If his work had weaknesses, they did not stem from a lack of scholarly dedication, but rather from his lack of scientific training as well as his insistence on the special status of man, an expected tenet in a religious leader. Still, his research on Darwinism was formidable. In his book, he covered almost all the major representatives of the school of evolution as well as some classical Arab writings. It is surprising that despite his serious efforts Isfahani's work on Darwinism has been inadequately read or considered. If the works of Arab scholars in Cairo were the main source of the Arab version of Darwinism, Isfahani and others, such as al-Zahawi (1863–1936), were their counterparts in Baghdad. It is also noteworthy that *al-Muqtataf*, the champion of Darwinism in the Arab world, never mentioned Isfahani's work on evolution. This circumstance, more than any other, leads us to conclude that the editor of *al-Muqtataf* sought to publish material that closely conformed to his own line of thought.

Isfahani was concerned with Darwin's theory as part of Western thought in general. He was certainly impatient with those who criticized Darwin, finding such authors not far removed from the materialists who gave various interpretations of evolution. Scientific agnosticism, as with Lamarck and Spencer, was considered a result of the ignorance of the researcher. But when a study clearly substituted natural laws for God, as in the cases of Büchner and Shumayyil, it was referred to as a consequence of atheist views.

Isfahani insisted on scientific evidence as a condition of proof. But, one might ask Isfahani, can we apply the same test to religion, which obviously could not be tested experimentally? Most probably his answer would be an uncompromising one. He would not dilute his religious convictions with a materialistic creed. Like Cheikho, he wanted to install religion as the sole arbiter of human knowledge. He rejected the notion that the nature of the material world could differ from that of the spiritual one. He seems not to have used the argument that, although we can test material forms in a laboratory, religious and spiritual questions are beyond material judgement.

The insistence in Arab religious circles on clear-cut empirical evidence to qualify Darwin's ideas as true science served to focus the important and controversial question of what constitutes science.

Could religious texts be qualified as true science, while evolutionist ideas were apocryphal science? As Thomas Kuhn has noted, there are, indeed, certain degrees of dogmatism about core commitments in scientific research. Kuhn has argued that such dogmatism plays a constructive role in promoting the aims of science. Scientists have been known to change their minds as well as persist in their views even if the views are not supported by experiments. The difference between the dogmatism of scientists and that exhibited by Muslim writers on Darwin is indeed very great. Yet in the light of current understanding about the history of science, the Muslim writers appear as informed and not unreasonable commentators on the nature of Western science.

MUSTAFA HASANAYN AL-MANSURI

Al-Mansuri, a Muslim scholar from Egypt, published a book on *Tarikh al-Madhahib al-Ishtirakiyah* (The History of Socialist Doctrine) in 1914 in which he devoted a chapter to Darwin's Doctrine and Socialism.[101] The central thesis of the chapter was that Darwin's ideas marked a new departure in human affairs. Mansuri, convinced of the validity of Darwin's science, asserted that Darwin 'completely destroyed the realm of doubts and illusions and gave rise to the natural laws which govern all living organisms'.[102]

Mansuri, unlike Hussein and Afghani, was mainly concerned with harmonizing science with religion. To make Darwinism acceptable, he wrote that Darwin's ideas were incorrectly equated with atheism and falsely described as irreligious. He noted that evolutionary thought did not contradict religion, and the evolution of living species from one origin, as explained by Darwin, did not deny God. In his own words, 'nothing in natural sciences can oppose religion; on the contrary they support it'.[103] He quoted Spencer's and Wallace's remarks on this issue. According to Spencer, 'Knowing natural science is a silent worship', and to Wallace, 'The adoption of natural science with the denial of one existence who controls [this world] is mere nonsense.'[104] While Wallace's views on religion had not been disputed by Arab thinkers, the author's attempt to portray Spencer, the non-believer, as a religious man, resemble Isfahani's effort. By doing so, both wished to reduce the tension between science and religion.

Mansuri was sure that the development of science would support traditional religion. In this respect, he saw more immediate perils to religion coming from those who added to the original ideas of religion rather than from scientists. He asserted:

> If a social reformer called for a cancellation of the budget alloca-
> tion for religious prayers, this is not an indication of atheism, but
> rather a social program to channel these expenses to education or
> building houses and hospitals for the benefit of the poor; prayers
> could be practiced at any location.[105]

Influenced by socialist ideas, the author went on to apply Darwin's ideas of natural selection and the survival of the fittest. He admitted that although competition among individuals causes hardships, it also stimulates individuals to strive for the best. Socialists were not totally against competition, but they wanted competition confined among workers and farmers for the purpose of upgrading one's mind; the individual worker would be induced to work not only to be victori-ous, but also to perform his duties well.[106] Mansuri held that Dar-win's natural selection was based on Thomas Malthus' theory of population growth. He was reluctant to accept the theory in its totality, however, for he wrote that the earth could sustain popula-tion growth if man uses his land efficiently, cultivates the unused part of the earth, if there were government legislation to limit birth, and if individuals refrained from polygamy and marriage at an early age.[107] The suggestions made by Mansuri criticised basic traditional social values. He preferred to see young Arabs marry at a later age and be restricted to one wife. This line of thought conformed to the line of certain Arab thinkers, such as Qasim Amin, the champion of wo-men's liberation.

Mansuri defended socialism because it did not obstruct natural processes by making the weak more competitive at the expense of the strong; socialism strove for equal opportunity among all workers. Socialism would lend support to natural selection by eliminating the principle of inheritance, where the sons of the rich, who could not survive without their parents support, would be eliminated.[108] This observation brought Mansuri to discuss the link between natural selection and socialism. He differentiated between what he called natural and artificial inheritance. In the former, he said, the father produced a healthy child because he was healthy, in the latter, the father left his child accumulated wealth which he collected by illegal means. Mansuri pointed out that artificial inheritance could not pass on to children not only because the father had no right to it in the first place, but also because it contradicts basic natural laws. Economic freedom stipulated the equality of all individuals; natural laws only distinguish humans by their natural, not their artificial, characteristics.[109]

While Mansuri credited the beneficial effects of competition and natural selection to social development, this observation was not an original one. Like Shumayyil, Musa and others, Mansuri acclaimed Darwin's evolution with enthusiasm for its liberating effect on traditional Arab culture. Mansuri accepted Darwin's theory with the same conviction as his Christian Arab secularist counterpart had demonstrated. He defended Darwin against his critics and wondered if the existing reward system for an inventor or discoverer was possibly enough to compensate Darwin, who had 'transformed the way scientists viewed the world' and thus 'changed the face of science altogether'. He added, 'was there, in this world, anyone who could financially reward Darwin or his inheritors with an amount equal to his contribution to knowledge?'[110] To portray Darwin's position in the chain of scientific development, he provided the following example. When monkeys saw a piece of food floating in a river and were afraid to pick it up, they climbed on a tree, formed a chain by holding on to each other's tails and in this way picked up the food for division among the entire tribe. Darwin's position resembled the role played by the monkey who first grasped the food.[111]

Despite Mansuri's short discussion of Darwinism, he exhibited a strong faith in the laws of evolution, and he applied them to criticize the ills of Egyptian society. Mansuri drew on Darwin to adapt the struggle for existence and survival of the fittest to shape Egyptian social life. Mansuri seriously attempted to marry Darwinism with religion.

HASSAN HUSSEIN

Hussein was a Muslim scholar from Egypt who in 1924 translated Ernst Haeckel's book on evolution into Arabic. The book appeared as *Fasil al-Maqal fi Falsafat al-Nushu wa-al-Irtiqa* (On the Philosophy of Evolution and Progress).[112]

Hussein introduced his translation with 72 pages on the philosophical and biological implications of evolution. He agreed with some of the scientific ideas propagated by Haeckel, but refuted all other ideas that contradicted religion and the existence of God. Unlike Shumayyil, who also had translated Büchner, Hussein was a committed believer in religion, God and spirit.[113] Hussein pointed out that while Haeckel followed the steps of eighteenth-century materialism, such as the ideas of d'Holbach, he echoed the writing of Arab thinkers and tradition to support religious convictions. This method of reviving and exploring the original ideas of Eastern philosophy in the light of modern thought, as we have seen, was common among Arab writers.

It is natural to ask, in view of these circumstances, why the author translated atheist material for Arab readers. Hussein's answer came in two parts: first, because the modern age is the era of evolution and change, and so it was necessary to introduce the Arabic reading public to recent views on the law of evolution; second, the Arabs badly needed to know modern scientific principles to advance materially. Unhappy about the largely unfruitful methods of debate among scholars, he wished to seize on 'the opportunity for us [the Arabs] to know about the methods of pure scientific research'.[114] He explained that neither Arab religion (Islam and Christianity) nor the Arab mentality prevents Arabs from understanding modern scientific thought. To support his view, Hussein sprinkled his introduction with verses from the Bible and Quran.

Hussein revealed two grounds on which he initially hesitated to translate Haeckel's book. First, Haeckel 'adopted a pure Darwinist view, and people hate even the mention of Darwin's name, for his ideas are interpreted to mean the denial of God's existence and the support of materialistic doctrine'. The second ground was that Haeckel attacked religion, especially Catholicism, 'an attack we categorically opposed'.[115] There is, of course, a hidden contradiction in Hussein's logic. At first, in the belief that Haeckel's ideas on evolution and materialism were worth translating, he provided his own evidence to discredit them. Later, he explained that ancient Arab philosophers originated the discussion of evolution. This obscurity of thought is no more than the result of an effort to link old Arab concepts to modern ideas. Hussein, along with most Muslim writers, felt that foreign ideas were basically unsuited to Arab tradition.

Like other Arab thinkers who followed the Islamic intellectual tradition, Hussein, in his quest to reconcile religion with science, stressed that Islam was a tolerant and rational religion. As such, if there was a contradiction between divine laws (*al-Sharia*) and reason, the latter had to be adopted.[116] To support this point, Hussein discussed the writing of Ibn Rushd (Averroes), and sought to sum up the work of the Creator in the arrangement of the world.[117] Unfortunately, Hussein handled his source material uncritically. He erroneously attributed the above mentioned opinion to Ibn Sina (Avicenna), for example. This infelicity was not due to a printing. error, as would have been usual at that time, but rather to careless quotation. To be sure, of course, the title of his discussion was, 'Ibn Sina's Opinion' and in the course of his discussion, Hussein also referred explicitly to the 'President' (a title given by Arabs to Ibn Sina). Hussein also quoted Ibn Rushd on pages 10, 11, 12, 13 and 14 without providing sources. This omission was not a common practice. Isfahani, for example, also did not provide exact references for some of his source material, but he was explicit in drawing the attention of his readers to this fact. Hussein's dereliction received notice from his contemporaries. In the course of reviewing Hussein's translation, Ismail Mazhar revealed the title of the book of Ibn Rushd's, which Hussein used, *Fasl al-Maqal Fima Bayn al-Shariah Wa-al-Hikma min Itisal* (On the Relationship Between Canon Laws and Wisdom).[118] Mazhar commented that it was one of the weakest books written by Ibn Rushd, if, indeed, he really wrote it.[119]

In his introduction, Hussein, like Afghani, confused what Darwin wrote about the origin of life and the story of creation. After mentioning that some of Darwin's ideas were based on pure assumptions and guesswork, he quoted Darwin to the effect that living organisms had originated from five or six separate species through special creation.[120] Later, he added, Darwin also indicated that these species came from primitive forms provided by God with life. Hussein asked, 'How did life come to these primates? Did it fall from the sky?' He provided his own answer: 'Darwin said it is possible.'[121] As we know, however, Darwin avoided discussion of the origin of life in his *Origin of Species*. If we understand Hussein literally, then it was not Darwin who said that life fell to earth from the sky, but rather William Thomson, Lord Kelvin. Hussein summarized Darwin's doctrine under three assumptions: 1) spontaneous generation; 2) struggle for survival; and 3) natural selection.[122] As to the first, Hussein spoke about Darwin's ideas on the variations in individual species and added that 'some of the variations were known while others were still unknown'.[123] Yet the use of spontaneous generation to describe Darwin's theory is obviously mistaken. And although the variations between individuals in a species were well-known at that time, what was not known was the *cause* of the variations.[124] Hussein's aim to provide a clear exposition of Darwinism was not enhanced by such statements. Hussein was, simply, at sea with the science. He wrote, 'all production cells are the same in animals and in all plants. Also plants and animals have the same embryological tissues'.[125] Ismail Mazhar correctly rephrased the statement to have scientific meaning: 'The reproductive cell is the origin of life in both animals and plants; both plants and animals had living tissues for their embryos.'[126]

In his effort to provide a better explanation for the story of the creation of the universe, Hussein mentioned theories provided by philosophy and religion from antiquity to the present. day. He pointed out that history of creation as explained by the holy books, especially the Quran, conforms to evolution and modern science. Hussein quoted from the 'Holy Quran': 'A day with Allah is as a thousand years of what ye Reckon'[127] and 'A day whereof the span is fifty thousand years.'[128] The concept of 'days' in the above verses were not used in literal sense, Hussein insisted. It just denotes a very long time. In such a case, a day might be equal to thousands as well as fifty thousands of years. In this way, he added, the various stages in the evolution of the universe, as indicated by the evolutionists, could be accounted for.[129]

Hussein also wrote about the origin of man, as the origin is mentioned in the Quran. In his view certain passages lend support to the theory of evolution. For example, he quoted the following verse: 'We have created you [man] from dust, then from a clot, then from a little lump of flesh shapely and shapeless, that we may make it clear for you.'[130] It is, of course, relatively easy to find such passages. At other points in the Quran, which are not cited by Hussein, man is described as created from dust or mud (verses III:59; XVIII:37; and XXXV:11). Verse XXXV:11 reads: 'Allah created you from dust, then from a little fluid, then he made you pairs (the male and female).'[131] Hussein cited the work of Ikhwan al-Safa and al-Maarri, ancient Arab philosophers, whose writings on the subject, as we have seen, bore some similarity to nineteenth-century evolutionary thought.[132] The most accurate and perhaps convincing section of Hussein's introduction was on Lamarck's theory (the use and disuse of organs in the process of evolution of species). Yet when he discussed DeVries' ideas on mutation. he did not know the name of the tree which had attracted the attention of DeVries while he was walking in the outskirts of Amsterdam.[133]

In his refutation of materialism, Hussein did not provide new insight. Instead, he echoed the arguments of Isfahani and Cheikho on the subject. He relied on the convictions of those scientists who clearly accepted both religious teaching and scientific discoveries. Among others, he mentioned Pasteur, Harvey, Newton, Huxley and Wallace.

The weakest point in his generally weak introduction was the section of 'Arabs and the Doctrine of Evolution'. In it, Hussein, like Isfahani, discussed traditional Arab ideas on evolution and claimed that what Darwin called natural selection was called 'heavenly wisdom' (hikmah Ilahyya)[134] by the pseudonymous writers called 'Ikhwan al-Safa'. Hussein found no difference between what Darwin and Larmack wrote about evolution and what Arabs had said about it. He claimed that Darwin's *Origin* was nothing more than a 'collection of old opinions molded and refined in the light of modern discoveries'.[135]

Hussein's introduction cannot be recommended as an example of careful research bearing out its claims concerning the introduction of modern scientific methods to the Arab world. The study abounds in errors of scientific judgement, transliteration and misreading. It seems more than a coincidence, furthermore, that Hussein provided exactly the same ideas, and sometimes the same writings, as had been given in Isfahani's work on evolution. It is probable that the text was at the very least inspired by Afghani's refutation and Isfahani's book on Darwinism. Unlike Afghani, who wrote to clarify scientific points, though, Hussein wrote from religious motives.

ISMAIL MAZHAR

Mazhar constitutes the last thinker of our study group. Among Muslim writers who responded to Darwinism, Mazhar was undoubtedly the most scientific and creative. He belonged to Musa's generation and, like Musa, he was interested in modern scientific ideas. He came to study evolution, like Musa, from the writings of Shummayyil and Sarruf. He was the first, among Arabs, to publish the Arabic translation of the first five chapters of Darwin's *Origin of Species* in 1918, adding four more chapters in 1928. (A complete translation of the *Origin* appeared only in 1964.) He prefaced his translation with a long introduction. In addition, he also wrote a book on the theory of evolution in 1924.[136] While he issued many publications on a wide range of subjects, here we are mainly concerned with his work on evolution.[137]

Mazhar recalled that while he was reading philosophical literature, he came across Shumayyil's book and, upon reading it, 'a sweeping change beyond description emerged in my mind'.[138] Like Musa, he also came into contact with evolution through *al-Muqtataf* and its editor Sarruf. Mazhar was influenced by Auguste Comte's positivist philosophy. He called Comte's law of the three stages 'al-darajat al-thalath':

The biggest discovery ever achieved by the human mind. . . . Every branch of our knowledge must have passed through these three different states: first, theological; second, metaphysical; and third, positive.[139]

He considered the first stage a necessary step for the human mind to understand facts and investigate sources. He thought of the second stage as a link between the first and the third stage and considered the last stage to represent the acme of human thought.[140]

Given this background, it comes as no surprise to find that Mazhar viewed ancient Arab civilization as not having surpassed Comte's second stage. Arab civilization, according to Mazhar, remained at the metaphysical state and had not evolved to reach the positivist stage, the state of analysis of the critical spirit.[141] Despite the spread of many philosophical doctrines among ancient Arab and Muslim scholars as a result of the translation movement from Greek, there was no school of thought that could be associated with the names of, for instance, al-Farabi, Ibn Rushd or Ibn Sina. In fact, he maintained that philosophical doctrines remained confined to individuals. Ibn Rushd's philosophy became known as a philosophical school of thought only when modern Europe acquired his books and made use of them in the positivist stage of its scientific development. Arab contributions were meagre except in medicine, chemistry and botany; they remained descriptive and were sometimes confined to metaphysical explanations.[142] Given this background, the author asserted that the state of metaphysics was the one that Afghani had inherited from the Arabs. Indeed, the work of Afghani, he avowed, was a setback not only to the Arabs but also to the entire Eastern quest for freedom of thought. He considered Afghani's ideas harmful to Arab scientific development.

Mazhar was unhappy about the philosophical background of the

Urabi revolution in Egypt in 1882. He held that this revolution, though an important one, could not trigger the hidden intellectual thought of Egypt.[143] Compared with the French Revolution, he added, the Urabi movement had no real ideology. The author, disenchanted with Arab impractical and fatalistic mentality, urged Arabs to adopt the Western positivist and scientific civilization. Like other Arab secularists, he called for the adoption of the scientific method not only in formal education but also as a mode of life.[144]

Like Arab secularists, Mazhar did not pass unnoticed by Arab scholars. While it is outside the scope of this study to discuss this issue, it is sufficient to mention that Amin al-Khuli, an Arab living in Berlin, and Mustafa al-Shihabi, a prominent Muslim scholar from Syria, wrote in the pages of *al-Muqtataf* refutations of Mazhar's interpretation of Arab civilization.[145] Both writers defended Afghani and ancient Arab writings on the ground that they were not totally metaphysical and, as such, positivism was part and parcel of Arab scientific work. To support their arguments, both relied on some Western writing which, obviously, credited the important role of medieval Arab authors. The French Social physicist Gustave LeBon was cited to support this point of view.

Besides being an admirer of Western scientific thought, Mazhar was also an advocate of an idea associated with the West, freedom of thought. The motto of his journal, *al-Usur*, was 'Harrir Fikrak' (Liberate Your Thought) and was based on this concept. He linked the idea of freedom with progress and advancement. For him, man must be free in his thought, speech and even in his religious beliefs. Thus, Mazhar affirmed that man should also liberate himself from blind tradition and follow only reason, which analyses and criticizes every aspect of life.[146] This frame of mind brought him into conflict with traditionalists and reactionaries and resulted in the closure of his journal after the burning of his printing press.[147]

Unlike Musa and Shumayyil, Mazhar considered religion to be a personal relationship between the human being and God. He justified religion in the evolutional scheme of society. He wrote that the religious impulse was not to be refused. He considered religion as a natural answer to human needs at an early stage of the development of society. In this regard, he saw Islam as a revolution against ignorance. He added that while Islamic laws were suitable for the prevailing social conditions, they are incompatible with modern Arab society. Mazhar, whose aim was to bring harmony between modern knowledge and human religion, asserted that religion should be limited to the relationship of man with God.

To the essential question of the role of authority with regard to religion, Mazhar believed that matters of religion should be left without interference from human authority. The individual should be freed from other shackles of religious domination. It was no surprise, therefore, to find that Mazhar spared no effort in praising the Turkish revolution of Ataturk against traditional theology. This revolution, according to him, paved the way for the progress of the East and would bring the East very close to the West.[148] Unlike Urabi's revolution, he considered the Turkish revolution as a mutation in modern history. It was the result of many factors which, when combined, could constitute a philosophy that guided the thought and opinion of Eastern people. It resembled the Russian revolution in its style of writing and publication. He added that the Turkish revolution achieved two goals: it subdued the Asian spirit and it introduced the modern European mentality.[149]

Mazhar associated Darwin's evolution with the notion of progress, a notion that Darwin himself did not intend to emphasize. Mazhar's book, entitled *The Doctrine of Evolution and Progress*, could not have been more explicit in this regard. It consisted of 12 chapters and 342 pages. It was a comprehensive account of the nature of the universe from ancient Greece up to his time. The importance of the book can be seen in the wide-ranging discussion of what ancient and modern writers, both Arabs and non-Arabs, had written on evolution and materialism. The timing of his book gave it an advantage over other books published a generation earlier on the same subject. The controversy over Darwinism among Arabs had, to a degree, subsided. Both Shumayyil's translation of Büchner's evolution and Afghani's refutation of materialism were already widely studied and discussed by Arab intellectuals. Furthermore, the book was published after Mazhar, himself, had translated Darwin's *Origin of Species*. Mazhar's book was a new attempt at synthesizing Darwin's ideas. It was, in fact, not written for the general public, but rather for readers with previous knowledge of evolutionary concepts. It contained numerous scientific terms that he attempted to arabize. While this energetic attempt (and others like it) gave the Arabic language a great wealth of scientific terms, it would certainly have caused inconvenience to those who were not familiar with the ideas.

In his introduction, Mazhar wrote that his book could be regarded as a long introduction to his translation of the *Origin of Species*.[150] And since the doctrine of evolution and progress had great impact on other branches of modern knowledge, he felt that its study and translation was worth most of a man's life and effort. He added that scientific thought would serve as a tool to overcome traditional Arab thought.[151] Mazhar, as a positivist, pointed out that for many reasons Darwin's theory had generated philosophical confusion among Arab thinkers. Most Arab scholars, including Shumayyil (who derived from Darwin's theory a materialist ideology), identified materialism and Darwinism as similar concepts. The Shumayyil-Büchner viewpoint had become widespread. Mustafa al-Shihabi, for example, a prominent scholar, indicated that 'many materialists believe in a rational God . . . among them Darwin himself'.[152] Mazhar went against this current. He aimed to show that evolution need not necessarily be extrapolated to either a cosmological view of the universe or to the exclusion of religion. After referring to Darwin's *Origin*, Mazhar found that Darwin's principles in fact had no impact whatever on religious feeling.[153]

Mazhar devoted almost his entire book to criticizing Shumayyil, Büchner and Afghani on evolution and materialism. Criticism of the former related to their use of Darwin's theory to support a materialistic world view. He began by treating the notion of spontaneous generation as used by Büchner and Shumayyil. In his reading of Shumayyil's translation of Büchner's commentary on Darwin, Mazhar found that Büchner misread Darwin's ideas on the origin of living matter, because Büchner thought that Darwin did not have the courage to say that all species came from one origin. This obviously gave support to spontaneous generation. Mazhar challenged this judgement based on his reading of Darwin's *Origin of Species*. In his view, Büchner could only blame Darwin for saying that God blew life into several instead of one form of primate. Even the mere acceptance of spontaneous generation did not oppose the view that life originated from several forms, because if spontaneous generation did happen in one geographical area, it could also happen elsewhere. Mazhar recognized that Darwin's stand was not due to lack of courage, but to lack of evidence.[154]

Mazhar felt that Darwin and Büchner differed not on the doctrine of evolution as such, but on the materialistic idea of creation. Mazhar did not deny the occurrence of spontaneous generation, but he did say that this claim by the materialists was based on mere assumptions without empirical evidence. And if it were proven, Mazhar continued, the materialists still had to face the complex question of the secret of life and its creation.[155] Drawing on an article written by Wallace which appeared in the London *Daily News* in 1923, Mazhar wrote, 'Living organisms which consisted of cells should be able to divide and change themselves. What, then, is the hidden secret within the cells that makes them transform and evolve to become animals or plants?'[156] He concluded by insisting that the doctrine of evolution did not treat the ultimate nature of things (*Mahiyat*) and that the role of the materialists should be confined to the study of the natural laws of life, rather than to exploration of the nature of life itself. The latter was still a puzzle in nature.[157] Mazhar also drew the attention of his readers to the fact that certain concepts, like 'force' and 'matter', cannot be explained by science. These terms denote only hidden and abstract meanings.[158] In other words, the forces acting to produce variation among species were still unknown. This led him to contrast the views held by the materialists and the creationists on the origin of life. He wrote, 'They both started from an abstract force', and added, 'Since we do not know the nature of life, then what is the real difference between those who believe that life was created or those that claim that it created itself?'[159]

Like other Arab thinkers, Mazhar attacked Shumayyil's views on religion and natural sciences. We have seen that Shumayyil, while professing the survival of natural sciences, attacked religion as the cause of human suffering. Mazhar attributed Shumayyil's stand on religion to his materialistic ideas. He felt that Shumayyil aimed to substitute one religion with another, 'the worship of matter'.[160] While Shumayyil never undermined the importance of religion in the progress of nations, as Mazhar explained, Mazhar's contention with Shumayyil concentrated on the role of natural sciences in the development of society. We find Mazhar in favour of the development of both literary and scientific branches of knowledge. He wrote that the denial of literary work is a denial of human striving.[161]

Mazhar's stand on Afghani's refutation of materialism was unambiguous. He wrote that Afghani's work created confusion and doubt among the Arab population regarding the principles of natural science.[162] In his effort to remove this confusion, Mazhar provided a detailed account of Afghani's ideas on the subject. In Mazhar's view, Afghani's assessment of Darwin's work was based on discredited sources and word-of-mouth. He added that Afghani had never read any of Darwin's work, and his refutation represented an appeal to emotional rather than rational thinking.[163] While Afghani refused to accept the term 'chance' used by the materialists to support natural laws which were still unknown, Mazhar felt that the materialists' use of the term gave witness to the inability of the human mind to explain certain natural phenomena.[164] Mazhar found, indeed, two natures in human beings: one was abstract and beyond the capability of the human brain to explain, and the other could be explained by scientific methods.[165]

In his introduction of *The Origin of Species*, which amounted to a hundred pages, Mazhar provided a detailed account of ancient Arab writings on the idea of evolution.[166] After mentioning the contributions of Greek philosophers, Mazhar cited many passages from Arab sources.[167] He quoted, for example, Ikhwan al-Safa, who discussed the close similarity between inorganic matter, plants and animals, and how they evolved from one another. Mazhar wrote that Haeckel's description of the 'Monera', the link between non-living and living matter, was similar to Ikhwan al-Safa's writing on 'khadra al-diman'.[168] He added that Arab scientists could have reached the same conclusions on evolution as modern scientists, if only they had had modern scientific equipment. Mazhar asserted that modern scientists would not be able to distinguish the botanical and animalistic characteristics of micro-organisms without the help of the modern microscope.[169] He mentioned the work of Ibn Miskawayh, Ibn Khaldun and others on the physical similarity between man and ape. He also touched on modern evolutionary writings, including Herbert Spencer's principles of evolution and progress and Darwin's ideas on heredity, the struggle for life and the survival of the fittest. Mazhar considered Darwin's theory on the descent of man the most probable explanation of the transformation of species, including man's descent from ape.[170]

THE MUSLIMS RECONSIDERED

Muslim thinkers interested in the reformist spirit of the age received the intellectual challenge of Darwinism with great concern. Jamal al-Din Afghani was the first to attack Darwin and the materialists who applied his theory outside its biological domain. Afghani's attack was a simplistic one and was not adequate to explain the essence of Darwinism. Hussein al-Jisr, Muhammad Rida Isfahani, Ismail Mazhar and al-Mansuri made serious efforts to adapt Darwinian evolution to the needs of the Muslim community. Hussein Al-Jisr, for example, asserted that whenever conclusive scientific evidence emerged, reinterpretation of religious dogma was necessary to justify the new reality.

Having seen how Muslim scholars received Darwin's ideas, let us see how Western writers viewed the Arab reception. The philosopher of biology David L. Hull, in his discussion of 'Darwinism and Historiography', mentioned that Darwinism was viewed by Muslims as a Christian heresy, since the Darwinians tended to be Christians.[171] In his remarks, Hull mentioned neither his sources nor whether these Christians were Arabs or Western writers. In the present study, which covers the major works published by both Christian and Muslim Arabs on Darwinism, there is no reference whatever to any Christian heresy. In fact, Louis Cheikho, the Jesuit, was the strongest advocate of anti-Darwinist polemics. While it is true that Afghani rejected Darwinism, al-Mansuri and Mazhar endorsed Darwin's ideas *in toto*, and there is no indication that al-Jisr or Isfahani rejected the same theory.

Some scholars have claimed that modern science was alien to the Muslim mind and that it affected only Christian Arabs whose interest, as a minority, was well served by it. The findings of the present study seem to discredit this opinion. Muslim thinkers accepted Darwin's theory, by and large, as an indication of natural laws which were subject to the wisdom and will of God. All in all, Muslim intellectuals received Darwinism with as great an interest as did their Christian counterparts. They immediately focused on a query that Darwinians posed to their society. Muslim writers suggested adapting the new ideas to their religious needs. In doing so, they provided a religious sanction to Darwin's science.

Najm Bezirgan has claimed that the failure of conservative Christian Arabs to create an anti-Darwinist front in the Arab world was due partly to the fact they were not noted religious or political leaders, but mostly because they were not Muslims.[172] As far as it goes, this claim is true. Yet Bezirgan did not take into account the comprehensive writings of Isfahani and al-Jisr on the subject. Both were prominent religious Shiite leaders. The Arab failure to create such a front more probably related to the increasing threat of Western economic and political domination. At the same time, as shown in this study, both the religious Muslim and the Christian drew on each other's writings to defend religion in general against Darwinism. The Muslim religious publications on Darwin's theory were mentioned in religious-oriented periodicals and not in the liberal Arab journals. Indeed, without the comment provided by *al-Mashriq* on Isfahani's work, it would be difficult for a traditional-minded Western scholar to appreciate his significance.

An author's religion was of secondary importance in the debate over Darwinism. Rather, it was largely a debate between religious men on the one hand and secularists on the other. The parties were mainly interested in the conflict between religious and materialistic interpretations of evolutionary thought. The doctrinal differences between Shiites and Sunnites, so important in political history, played no role in shaping the argument against Darwinism.

Conclusion

This study has presented the thoughts of Arab writers, both Christians and Muslims, on Darwin's theory of evolution. It has demonstrated how Darwinism, as a Western scientific idea, was greatly discussed and debated among Arab thinkers who were responding to the impact of Western thought. Arab reaction to Darwinism came at a time when secular-rational ideas were already known among the educated segment of population. The writings of both Muslims and Christians, radical and conservative, remained rooted in the philosophical, social and religious aspects of Darwinism. While it is obvious that biological evolution was not the main concern of Arab thinkers, they demonstrated a wide diversity of thought about evolutionary ideas. This diversity of thinking did not elaborate on Darwinism, as such. Arab writers neither introduced original ideas on the subject nor did they produce scientific research of their own. Nevertheless, the earliest Arab responses to Darwinism during the late nineteenth century came at just about the same time that the battle over almost the same issues was being conducted by Westerners.

The Arab world began to develop an interest in modern science and a sense of national pride during the second half of the nineteenth century. There was a new commitment to overcome backwardness in science, which had been endemic under Ottoman rule. Overcoming oppressive and bureaucratic Ottoman obstacles was one of the conditions of success for any scientific undertaking. While it is true that the Arab response to Darwinism reflected Western rather than specifically Arab issues, Arab interest was not primarily the result of concern with biological sciences. It was instead the logical outcome of the role played by the natural sciences in radical Arab thought. Many Arab scholars hoped to undermine repressive Ottoman rule by the widespread transmission of the modern ideas of natural sciences, including Darwin's theory of evolution. They felt that through the introduction of scientific principles an Arab awakening could be brought about.

Shumayyil found in Darwinism the key to his materialistic view of the universe. For Shumayyil and Musa, Darwin's theory provided an explanation of the organic world without resort to a Creator in general. Arab secularists, both Christian and Muslim, received Darwin's idea with great enthusiasm. They found it the symbol of progressive development and the kernel of all sciences. Arab secularists exaggerated the importance of Darwin's theory, but conservative elements also overestimated the impact of Darwin's struggle for survival without realizing that Darwin had used the idea only in a metaphorical sense. The debate between Mazhar and Hussein, the Deputy Minister of Education of Egypt, on the meaning of natural selection and survival of the fittest, is a case in point.

It is clear from this study that there was one obvious difference between Muslim and Christian secularist writers. While both camps were in agreement in accepting Darwin's evolutionary thought as a scientific doctrine, they disagreed in their specific interpretations. Mazhar and al-Mansuri, the Muslims, viewed Darwinism as essentially in accord with religious teaching. Musa, the Christian, aimed to destroy all religious establishments. Yet all Arab secularists rejected the applications of Darwin's ideas by Europeans to support racial conflict and justification of war. The debate between Sarruf, Shumayyil and others on materialism and war exhibits this unanimity.

Shumayyil was the first to introduce Darwinism and materialism into the Arab world. His translation of Ludwig Büchner's work on Darwinism clarified his materialistic and atheist inclinations. While scientific research left little room for the idea of spontaneous generation, Shumayyil continued to defend the idea, based on his faith in the forces of matter. Unlike radical Arab writers, Sarruf was moderate in his stand on Darwinism. Through his journal *al-Muqtataf*, he attempted to transmit Western scientific thought, especially Darwinism, in a very careful manner. Sarruf was a divine-evolutionist who rejected materialism.

The call by some Arabs for the complete adoption of Western civilisation, which they regarded as a combination of ancient cultures, including the Arab one, made Western culture seem to be a universal one. This universalistic view of European civilization by the Arabs discredited the division provided by Kipling between East and West.

Unlike Arab religious thinkers, who viewed modern scientific development as a support for rather than a threat to established religion, Arab secularists were never at ease with religion and its impact on traditional values when faced with the new ideas of science. In this respect, Arab secularists, whether Muslim or Christian, assimilated Darwin's ideas easily and viewed them as the mechanism for Arab progress and development. Opposition to these ideas came from religious circles, both Christian and Muslim. As a group, Arab secularists could be viewed as more open to Western ideas than were Arab religious thinkers. The religion of a thinker was less important than his broader ideological commitment.

Arab religious thinkers, both Muslim and Christian, attacked Darwinism on purely religious grounds. They argued that religious texts were not religious dogma, but an alternative source to the ever-changing assumptions, theories and interpretations offered by science. They advocated their views not as believers but as scientists engaged in scholarly debate about the validity of a scientific theory, namely Darwin's evolution. The debate over Darwinism was part of the Arab intellectual revival, reflecting a quest for order and authority in an Arab society that was increasingly influenced by Western thought.

Muslim religious writers, except for Afghani, were not against evolution, although they warned against the uncritical acceptance of Darwin's ideas. They interpreted the theory of evolution in terms of Quranic authority. Muslim thinkers attempted to read into Islam some of the non-Islamic and non-theistic concepts of modern science and asserted that these concepts really had roots in Islam. Although the Quran is not a scientific or biological book and refers to natural phenomena by way of accident, Muslim thinkers, such as Isfahani, al-Jisr and Hussein, were successful in finding Quranic verses that supported the wisdom of God in creating the universe, and these verses were not as mythical and irrational as one might have expected. They pointed out that Islam is generally more rational and sounder than many of the interpretations offered by scientists.

Afghani completed a philosophical work against Darwinism in 1881. His belief in Islamic thought led him to view Darwin's ideas on creation and variation in species as only a meaningless mass of doubts and guesswork. Moreover, Afghani found Darwin's theory, as well as materialistic thought, to be completely indigestible. He insisted that God's purpose and wisdom in creating life on earth is responsible for the differentiation of species and that Darwin's natural selection was not a factor in the evolutionary process.

Hussein al-Jisr, a conservative and religious thinker, wrote another philosophical work in 1887 on materialism and Darwinism. The result was that he attempted a reconciliation between Darwinism and Islam by providing an intelligent interpretation of the *Shariah* to suit modern scientific and biological principles. Al-Jisr even explained the essential harmony between materialism and Islam, based on his belief that there are certain natural phenomena which could be explained neither by science nor by materialistic ideas, and thus God is the Creator of such phenomena.

The major effect of Darwinism on Islamic thought, as on Christian Arab ideas, was to reinforce old beliefs rather than to develop new ones. This is a consequence of sociopolitical reality. In their discussion of Darwinism, Arab thinkers drew heavily on the writings of Western scholars because they did not have the stock of political and economic institutions that one found in the West. Under Ottoman rule, Arabs were not allowed freedom of intellectual expression. There was no scientific research, as such, in the Arab provinces of the Ottoman Empire.

The Arab version of Darwinism represents a unique case in the reception of a scientific theory. Almost all Arab thinkers of our study group referred to their ancestor's contributions on the subject. For instance, Afghani claimed that Darwin was a mere collector of ancient writings on evolution; others felt that Darwin did not provide any new insight on the subject, which was constituted by Arab ideas and work. In this confusion, Sarruf was well aware of Darwin's scientific contribution to the theory of evolution. He repeatedly asserted that ancient Arab writings were descriptive in nature and that it was Darwin who built the theory on rigorous grounds.

As a group, Arab religious thinkers asserted that the Quran and the Bible are the fountainhead of all knowledge, scientific or otherwise. The scientific output of the world, including modern discoveries and theories, were reduced to a mere fraction of the knowledge already embodied in the holy books. They regarded scientific inventions as revelations of the secrets of the universe created by God. Arab writers found many verses in the Quran that spoke about evolution. They concluded that evolution is not an anti-religious teaching. Isfahani and al-Jisr stated the case unambiguously.

This turn of mind accepted Darwin's science and attempted to reconcile it with religion. While a positive attitude to science lent support to progressive forces, it remained at the theoretical and apologetic level. Al-Jisr, for instance, stated that the principles of Islam are not opposed to true science. When a scientific concept emerged to contradict an Islamic principle, an interpretation of the concept had to be developed to conform with modern reality. Ignorant interpretations of Islamic laws, however, would be harmful to Islam, and should be avoided by those Muslims who knew nothing more than the observance of ritual and customs.

Arab religious thinkers contended with the idea of evolution to the extent that they felt that the idea did not agree with religious teaching. It was seen as not providing for God's wisdom in the creation of species, for example. If one uses the phrases 'evolution occurred by God's control' and 'universe was created for a purpose' and 'materialism is a neutral thought', one finds total support among Arab religious thinkers, Muslim and Christian. But for Shumayyil and Musa, these phrases would find outright rejection. Both agreed that supernatural forces had to be excluded from the natural process.

When science renounced traditional ideas, Arab religious thinkers accepted it as the main support for their views. And when science brought into focus the consonance of reasoning with reality, Arab religious writers resorted to miracles and other biblical episodes. Louis Cheikho stated this case very clearly. As a group, Arab religious scholars began to feel that the march of science was a fact of life and that literal interpretations of the holy books were becoming irrelevant. Still, when science drew attention to certain changes or to rejection of some of its own ideas as a result of new scientific knowledge, Arab religious men found merit in a religion that does not change and which contains all sciences. This line of thought served to widen rather than narrow the gap between science and religion.

Arab religious thinkers, both Muslim and Christian, were leaders of repute and therefore sought to place religion before science whenever the two disagreed. They could have limited their intellectual activity to their own sphere of work, but they chose to join the debate over Darwinism. They could have waited for the outcome of scientific research rather than depict Darwin's work as mere speculation and guesswork. Cheikho's controversies with Arab secularists on the meaning of biblical stories are of little value today. Nevertheless, Arab religious involvement in scientific debate over the issue of science and faith can be understood on the grounds that it was inevitable for men of their time to defend any deterioration in the moral standard of the reading public. Thus the needs of the time, as they saw them, made it difficult for the Arab religious group to limit their contributions to the narrow range of their own expertise.

Were there any differences between Muslim and Christian Arab religious thinkers, concerning Darwin's theory of evolution? The answer is not difficult to find. While both were open to Darwinism, this study suggests that Muslims were more ready to accept Darwin's evolution than were the Christian Arabs. Although all Muslims except Afghani stated clearly that evolution as provided by Darwin was in agreement with the teaching of the Quran, Cheikho and other religious Christians were less open and more critical of Darwin's work. Yet both groups provided interpretations of the Quran and the Bible to accommodate Darwinism. While the Christian Arabs resorted to the miracles of the Bible, the Muslims, such as al-Jisr and Hussein, provided better and more rational interpretations of the Quran to reconcile Darwinism with religion. Here is a refutation to those who claim that Christian Arabs were more open than the Muslims in their reaction to Western ideas.

Arab religious groups of both faiths debated religion and science with Arab secularists. Their lasting contribution can be seen in the light of having made available to the reading public the methods and results of European writers. Together with other Arab thinkers, they helped to provide the intellectual stimulus and framework essential for the average reader to formulate his own appreciation of the importance of modern scientific ideas. Arab investigation into the ancient Arab sciences and history to accommodate the challenge posed by the liberal and scientific ideas of the West made the reader more aware of his own scientific heritage. The Arab-Islamic version of Darwinism added a special twist to the broader history of Darwin's evolution.

Arab writers who emphasized the work of their ancestors aimed, perhaps, to underline two points. First, they sought to praise past Arab scientific endeavours in order to overcome their present backwardness in science. Second, in doing so, they sought to find a solution to their chronic social problems.

The conditions which hindered the development of science still persist in the Arab world of today. Antoine Zahlan, in his work on Arab science policy, points out that while individual Arab scientists are capable of producing scientific work equal to their counterparts elsewhere in the world, their work does not lead to the development of science in the Arab world because they are part of a 'community that does not possess any of the appropriate cultural and institutional facilities to support them.'[1] Zahlan's high regard for Arab scientists led him to blame politicians and others, rather than the scientists themselves, for hindering the implantation of science and technology in the Arab world. Another study conducted by the author of the present dissertation lends support to Zahlan's finding. Arab scientists residing outside the Arab world, in North America, are as productive as and even more visible than American scientists.[2]

Having dealt at some length with the impact of Arab secular and religious thought on Darwinism, an essential question remains. Have scientists and theologians come to an accord on the nature of life and human existence? In other words, how does scientific research help to explain the principal issue of human creation and the mystery of life? The points raised in the second half of the nineteenth century about creation, man's intellectual faculties and providence still persist among modern thinkers and philosophers. The inability of science to provide concrete answers to these complex questions is not a victory of creationist forces but rather a result of the fact that science never stops changing in the light of new scientific discoveries. At the same time, science has left some old beliefs intact. The recent reaction by scientific creationists against evolution in the United States represents a clear manifestation that the reconciliation of Darwinism and religion still occupies the minds of not only religious men but also scientists, and this in a scientifically advanced country. In this regard, the Arab world seems unexceptional. In 1982, Dr Abd al-Muhsin Salih wrote an article entitled 'Al-Kashf an al-Halaqat al-Mafquda fi Nasb al-Insan' (On the Missing Link in Human Origin) which appeared in *Majallat al-Doha*.[3] In it, he praised those individuals who adopted the idea of special creation. He added that the gap between man and ape is so wide that it is impossible for man to have come from the same origin as the ape.[4]

While it is obvious that science has had a great impact on every aspect of our life and seems to pose a threat to religion and traditional values, still it may well be that science has never won the allegiance of the majority of the population. It may be an activity and a mode of thought for the educated few. Science may be doomed to come into conflict with religion as long as religion persists in the mind of the people and as long as science has not eradicated the uncertainties that seem to demand religious beliefs.

The present study is sufficient to shed some light on a point that has rarely been observed before. This point concerns the interest in Western scientific thought manifested by Arabs, both Christian and Muslim, throughout the nineteenth century. It seems safe to conclude that the traditional view in the history of science, where science in its post-seventeenth century form is held to be almost absent from the Arab collective mind before the twentieth century, can no longer be maintained with any degree of confidence.

Notes and References

1 INTRODUCTION

1. Philip Hitti, 'The Impact of the West on Syria and Lebanon in the Nineteenth Century', *Cahiers d'histoire mondiale*, 2 (1955), p. 610.
2. Ibid.
3. For more information on the history of Arab and Islamic education, see A. L. Tibawi, *Islamic Education* (London 1972); Roderic Mathews and M. Akrawi, *Education in Arab Countries of the Near East* (Washington 1949); Fahim Qabain, *Education and Science in the Arab World* (Baltimore 1966); Bayard Dodge, *Al-Azhar – A Millennium of Muslim Learning* (Washington 1961); James Heyworth-Dunne, *An Introduction to the History of Education in Modern Egypt* (London 1939); A. L. Abd-al-Karim, *Tarikh al-Talim fi Misr, 1848–1882* (Cairo 1917); Y. S. Kotb, *Science and Science Education in Egyptian Society* (New York 1951).
4. Zaydan, 'Tarikh al-Nahda al-Ilmiya al-Akhira' (The History of Recent Scientific Awakening), *al-Hilal*, 9 (1901), p. 202.
5. Tibawi, *Islamic Education*, p. 47.
6. Ibid., p. 49.
7. Heyworth-Dunne, *History of Education in Egypt*, pp. 77–87.
8. Zaydan, 'Tarikh al-Nahda al-Ilmiya', pp. 235–36. Tibawi indicated that Syria had more educational facilities than Egypt, which later counted fifty schools on the eve of the introduction of Western methods, Tibawi, *Islamic Education*, p. 48.
9. On the impact of the French Revolution on Arab and Turkish thought, see Raif Khori, *Al-Fikr al-Arbi al-Hadith* (Modern Arab Thought) (Beirut 1943); and L. Zolondek, 'The French Revolution in Arabic Literature of the Nineteenth Century', *The Muslim World*, 57 (July, 1967), pp. 202–11; B. Lewis, 'The Impact of the French Revolution on Turkey', *Journal of World History*, 1 (1953), pp. 105–25.
10. On Bulaq Press, see J. Heyworth-Dunne, 'Printing and Translation under Muhammed Ali of Egypt: The Foundation of Modern Arabic', *Journal of the Royal Asiatic Society*, 3 (London 1940), pp. 325–49.
11. Heyworth-Dunne, *History of Education in Egypt*, pp. 345–80.
12. On the translation movement, see, Ibrahim Abu-Lughod, *Arab Rediscovery of Europe* (Princeton 1963); J. al-Shayyal, *Tarikh al-Tarjama fi Asr Muhammad Ali* (Cairo 1951) (History of Translation Movement Under the Rule of Muhammad Ali).

131

13. For an examination of the first Egyptian student mission to France, see Alain Silvera, 'The First Egyptian Student Mission to France under Muhammad Ali', *Middle East Studies*, 16 (1980), pp. 1–22. For Turkish students sent to France, see the article by Richard L. Chambers in his collection *Beginnings of Modernization in the Middle East in the Nineteenth Century* (Chicago 1968).

14. Tibawi, *Islamic Education*, p. 64 and K. al-Yaziji, *Rowwad al-Nahda al-Adabiya* (Beirut 1962) (Pioneers of Literary Awakening), pp. 25–28.

15. On the history of Western press in Syria, see L. Cheikho, 'Tarikh Fan al-Tibaah fi al-Sharq', *al-Mashriq*, 3 (1900), pp. 251–57, 706–14, 800–7, 839–44; Hitti, 'The Impact of the West on Syria and Lebanon', *Cahiers d'histoire mondiale*, 2 (1955), p. 615.

16. Tibawi, *Islamic Education*, p. 64.

17. S. al-Rifaai, *Tarikh al-Sahafa al-Suriya* (History of Syrian Press) (Cairo 1967), p. 100.

18. Philip Tarazi, *Tarikh al-Sahafa al-Arabiya* (Beirut 1913), 4 vols (hereafter cited as *Tarikh al-Sahafa*) and Zaydan, 'Tarikh al-Nahda al-Sahafiya' (History of Awakening Press), *al-Hilal*, 7 (1898), pp. 483–92.

19. On this decision see H. Jessup, *Fifty-Three Years in Syria* (New York 1910), vol. 2, pp. 707–8.

20. J. Zaydan *Tarajim Mashahir al-Sharq* (Cairo 1902), pp. 27–34 (hereafter cited as *Tarajim*).

21. Ibid., pp. 22–26.

22. Quoted in Hisham Sharabi, 'The Burden of the Intellectuals of the "Liberal Age"', *Middle East Journal*, 20 (1966), p. 228. For Tahtawi's influence and a list of his works, see Ahmad Badawi, *Rifat al-Tahtawi Bey* (Cairo n.d.), pp. 87–92, 93–149, and Zaydan, *Tarajim*, pp. 22–26.

23. On the history and aims of the SPC: *al-Muqtataf*, 3 (1878), pp. 113–15; ibid. 9 (1885), pp. 633–36; 24 (1904), pp. 866–69 and H. Jessup, *Fifty-Three Years in Syria* (New York 1910), 2 vols. John Munro, *A Mutual Concern – The Story of the American University of Beirut* (New York 1977). Faith Hanna, *An American Mission* (Boston 1979); F. J. Bliss, *The Reminiscenses of Danial Bliss* (New York 1920); S. P. L. Penrose, *That They May Have Life* (New York 1941). On the history and publication of St Joseph University, see Cheikho's series of articles *al-Mashriq*, 26 (1923), pp. 478–93, and the subsequent years on the University Jubilee, 1924 to 1927.

24. George Antonius, *The Arab Awakening* (London 1938), p. 35.

25. L. Cheikho, *Al-Adab al-Arabiya fi al-Qarn al-Tasa Ashar* (Beirut 1908, 4 vols) (Arabic Literature of Nineteenth Century), vol. 1, pp. 47–75.

26. Quoted in Ahmad Seraj al-Din, 'Al-Haraka al-Tarbawya fi Lubnan wa Suria' (Educational Movement in Lebanon and Syria), *al-Abhath*, 19 (1966), p. 333. Throughout this study, all translations are mine, unless otherwise indicated.

27. The representative of this school is George Antonius, *Arab Awakening*, p. 42.

28. A. L. Tibawi, *A Modern History of Syria* (Edinburgh 1969), p. 142.

29. K. al-Yaziji, *Rowwad al-Nahda al-Arabiya* (Beirut 1962), p. 107.

30. Ibid. pp. 107–8.

31. Yusuf Sarkis, a well-known Arab biographer mentioned that a Lebanese by the name of Ibrahim al-Najjar (1822–1864) who studied medicine in Egypt and graduated in 1842 was appointed as a Military Medical Doctor in Beirut. Yusuf I. Sarkis, *Muajm al-Matbuat al-Arabiyya wa al-Muarraba* (Cairo 1921–31), vol. 1, p. 21 (hereafter cited as *Muajm al-Matbuat*).
32. For the summary of these books, see J. al-Shayyal, *Tarikh al-Tarjamah*, appendix one, pp. 6–28.
33. L. Cheikho, 'Ubil Kulliatuna al-Fidi' (The Silver Jubilee of Our College), *al-Mashriq*, 4 (1901), p. 8. Cheikho also wrote on the Golden Jubilee of the College and named 760 medical doctors who graduated from the college during the years 1875–1925. *Al-Mashriq*, 23 (1925), p. 332.
34. *Al-Muqtataf*, 20 (1896), p. 217.
35. Cornelius van Dyck (1818–1895) was born in New York where he graduated from medical school. He came to Beirut in 1840 as an American missionary. As part of his work as a medical doctor, van Dyck was active in establishing schools in Syria. When the SPC was founded in 1866, he was appointed a professor of medicine and remained so until his resignation in 1882. Van Dyck wrote many scientific books on chemistry, physics, astronomy and, of course, medical texts. He helped in the translation of the Bible into Arabic. See J. Zaydan, *Tarajim Mashahir*, pp. 45–51. For more discussion on his life and work, see *al-Muqtataf*, 9 (1884), pp. 120–21; Yusuf Khouri, 'Cornelius van Dyck: Mualafatuh al-Ilmiya' (his scientific work), *Al-Abhath*, 18 (1965), pp. 389–418. Lutfi M. Saadi, 'Al-Hakim Cornelius van Allen van Dyck (1818–1895)', *Isis*, 27 (1937), pp. 20–45.
36. William van Dyck (1857–1939), third son of Cornelius van Dyck, joined the teaching staff of the Medical School of the SPC in 1880. Like his father, he was very active in promoting science among the Syrian population. He contributed many scientific articles to *al-Muqtataf* and brought Darwin's books with him to Beirut. He resigned in 1882 but went back to the SPC to teach medicine in 1918, where he remained until 1923. See Nadia Farag, *Al Muqtataf 1876–1900: A Study of the Influence of Victorian Thought on Modern Arabic Thought* (unpublished Ph.D. dissertation, University of Oxford, 1969), p. 75 (hereafter cited as *Influence of Victorian Thought on Arabic Thought*).
37. On his life and work, see Zaydan, *Tarajim* pp. 239–42; Tarazi, *Tarikh al-Sahafa*, pp. 116–19; Lutfi M. Saadi, 'The Life and Work of George Edward Post (1838–1909)', *Isis*, 28 (1938), pp. 385–417, *al-Hilal*, 18 (1910), pp. 222–26.
38. This information is chosen from the *Biographical Dictionary of Scientists*, ed. T. L. Williams, A. and C. Black (London 1974), and the various editions of *J. C. Poggendorff's biographisch-literarishes Handwörterbuch*.
39. On the publications of the staff members of the SPC, see Suha Tamim, *Bibliography of AUB Faculty Publications 1866–1966* (Beirut 1967).
40. Antonius, *Arab Awakening*, p. 51 see also Zaydan, *Tarikh Adab al-Lughah al-Arabiyah* (Cairo 1911, 4 vols), vol. 4, p. 79 (hereafter cited as *Tarikh Adab*).

41. Quoted by Fuad Sarruf, 'Tatawwar al-Fikr al-Ilmi fi Miat Sana' (The Development of Arab Scientific Thought) in *Nashat al-Arab al-Ilmi fi Miat Sana* (Beirut 1963), (Arab Scientific Thought in a Hundred Years), pp. 404–5.

42. Yusuf Sarkis, 'Al-jamaya al-Mashriqya fi Beirut' (Oriental Society in Beirut), *al-Mashriq*, 12 (1909), pp. 32–38.

43. On its activities and membership, see Zaydan, *Tarikh Adab*, vol. 4, pp. 80–81; Antonius, *Arab Awakening*, pp. 53–54.

44. On the society al-Majma al-Ilmi al-Sharqi, see Zaydan, *Tarikh Adab*, p. 85. The meetings of this society were reported in *al-Muqtataf*, for example, 6 (1882), p. 304; 8 (1883), pp. 529–34

45. See Zaydan, *Tarikh Adab*, p. 85.

46. *Al-Muqtataf*, 7 (1883), p. 254. For more industrial and agricultural information, see *al-Muqtataf*, 7 (1883), p. 193, pp. 336–38.

47. Shams al-Birr, founded in 1869 in Beirut as a branch of the British YMCA. Many of its members graduated from the SPC, including Nimr, Sarruf and Zaydan. See Zaydan, *Tarikh Adab*, vol. 4, pp. 81–82. On Nimr discussion, see *al-Muqtataf*, 7 (1883), pp. 262–68.

48. For more information on the activities of these societies and others, see Zaydan, *Tarikh Adab*, pp. 82–89.

49. On the history and the activity of this institute, see Zaydan, *Tarikh Adab*, p. 93. Cheikho, 'Kitab al–Dhab' (On Golden Jubilee of the Egyptian Scientific Society), *al-Mashriq*, 3 (1900), pp. 193–201. Tawfic Iskarus, 'Maahad Misr al-Ilmi', *al-Hilal*, 21 (1921), pp. 579–87.

50. On this society see, *Le Livre d'Or de l'Institut égyptien, publié à l'occasion du Centenaire de la fondation de l'Institut d'Egypte* (Le Mans 1899).

51. On the activity of the Geological society, *al-Muqtataf*, 10 (1886), p. 509; 13 (1888), p. 210; 15 (1891), p. 347; 19 (1895), p. 318; 21 (1897), p. 318; 66 (1925), p. 135; Zaydan, *Tarikh Adab*, p. 90. On its jubilee, see editorial comments, *al-Majlla al-Shahriya*, 1 (1925), pp. 189–93. On the Agricultural Society, *al-Muqtataf*, 30 (1905), p. 77; 32 (1907), p. 151; 38 (1922), p. 179.

52. On the beginning of the Arab Press, see Tarazi, *Tarikh al-Sahafa*, vol. 1, pp. 1–69. *Al-Hilal*, 6 (1898), pp. 483–92. The best survey of Arab periodicals is provided in Martin Hartmann's *The Arabic Press in Egypt* (London 1899.)

53. Tarazi, *Tarikh al-Sahafa*, vol. 1, p. 6.

54. Ibid.

55. A. Ahmed-Bioud, *3200 Revues et journaux arab*.

56. On the impact of *al-Muqtataf*, see Farag, *Influence of Victorian Thought on Arabic Thought*, pp. 57–118.

57. Ibid., p. 2.

58. Quoted in *al-Muqtataf*, 7 (1882), p. 249.

59. On his work, Hourani, *Arabic Thought*, pp. 246–247. Thomas Phillip, *Gurgi Zaidan: His Life and Thought* (Beirut and Wiesbaden 1979).

60. J. Zaydan, *Tarikh al-Tamaddun al-Islami* (Cairo 1902); Zaydan, *Al-Arab Qabl al-Islam* (Cairo 1908); Zaydan, *Tarikh Adab al-Lughah al-Arabiyah* (Cairo 1911).

61. The life and work of the last three authors is still unknown to me. This

biographical information is based on Zirkili's biographical dictionary, *Al-Alam* (Cairo 1954–59), vol. IX; Zaydan, Tarajim Mashahir al-*Sharq*, pp. 52–61; Tarazi, *Tarikh al-Sahafa al-Arabiya*, pp. 293–99.

62. Although Afghani was not an Arab, his work had a great impact on Arab intellectuals and for this reason he was considered in this study. For the list of his publications, A. Albert Kudsi-Zadeh, *Middle Eastern Studies*, 2 (October 1965), pp. 66–72. For his general ideas, M. al-Makhzumi, *Khatirat Jamal al-Din* (Beirut 1931) (Thought of Jamal al-Din).

63. For his political activities, Nikki R. Keddie, *Sayyid Jamal al-Din al-Afghani: A Political Biography*(Berkeley 1971); S. al-Shahrestani, 'Al-Sayyid Jamal al-Din al-Asaadabadi', *al-Irfan*, 24 (1933), pp. 58–68, 235–40.

64. The translation of *The Refutation* from the original Persian into English can be found in N. Keddie, *An Islamic Response to Imperialism* (Berkeley 1968), pp. 130–74 (hereafter cited as *Islamic Response*).

65. On Abduh's ideas, see Charles C. Adams, *Islam and Modernism in Egypt* (London 1933), pp. 104–74 and Hourani, *Arabic Thought*, pp. 130–60.

66. He had great influence, for example, on Rashid Rida, who wrote a book on Abduh, *Tarikh al-Ustadh al-Shaykh Muhammad Abduh* (History of Muhammad Abduh) (Cairo 1907).

67. Hourani, *Arabic Thought*, p. 144.

68. On his life and work Daghir, *Masadir al-Dirasat*, vol. 2, pp. 270–72.

69. Ibid., p. 270.

70. Ibid.

71. Hourani, *Arabic Thought*, pp. 222–24.

72. For his biographical information, Daghir, *Masadir al-Dirasat*, vol. 2, pp. 540–49; Tarazi, *Tarikh al-Sahafa*, vol. 4, pp. 124–29. See also *al-Muqtataf* issues of 1927–28, which were mostly dedicated to Sarruf's life and work especially 72 (1928), pp. 155–58, 287–92; 73 (1928), pp. 137–42, 187–90, 429–39.

73. Daghir, p. 540.

74. Ibid., p. 541–42.

75. For his life and work, Daghir, *Masadir al-Dirasat*, vol. 3, p. 1352; Tarazi, *Tarikh al-Sahafa*, vol. 4, pp. 138–42.

76. S. Penrose, *That They May Have Life: The Story of the American University of Beirut* (New York 1941), p. 70 and *Al-Hilal*, 25 (1917), pp. 422–26.

77. For biographical information on Shumayyil: Daghir, *Masadir al-Dirasat*, pp. 497–500; *al-Muqtataf*, 50 (1917), pp. 105–12, 225–31.

78. Y. Sarruf 'Dr. Shibli Shumayyil', *al-Muqtataf*, 50 (1917), p. 107.

79. Penrose, *That They May Have Life*, p. 33.

80. M. Hartmann, *The Arabic Press of Egypt*, pp. 66–67. Zaydan, *Tarikh Adab*, vol. 4, p. 73. *Al-Shifa* is considered the first medical journal in Arabic, but in my research, I found an earlier medical periodical, *Yacoub al-Tib*, published by M. Ali.

81. For his contribution to *al-Muqtataf*, *Fihrist al-Muqtataf* (Beirut 1968), vol. 2, pp. 339–41.

82. Republished in *Falsafat al-Nushu wa al-Irtiqa* (Cairo 1910), pp. 63–224.

83. Some parts of this book were published in *al-Muqtataf*, 4 (1879), pp. 41–43, 65–67, 98–100, 125–27.
84. For biographical data, Daghir, *Masadir al-Dirasat*, vol. 2, pp. 515–24.
85. Ibid., p. 516.
86. On the list of his publication, ibid., pp. 517–22.
87. M. Kurd Ali, 'Al-Ustad al-Aab Louis Cheikho', *Amal al-Majma al-Ilmi al-Arabi*, 8 (1928), pp. 231–35.
88. Published in Cairo in 1947 and translated into English by L. Schuman, *The Education of Salama Musa* (Leiden 1961).
89. S. Musa, *Tarbiyat Salama Musa* (Cairo 1947).
90. See the annotated bibliography of Musa in Daghir, *Masadir al-Dirasat*, vol. 2, pp. 553–56.
91. Musa, *Tarbiyat Salama*, p. 242. Reference will be made to Musa's other work only when it has bearing on our study.
92. On his life and work, Daghir, *Masadir al-Dirasat*, vol. 3, pp. 1237–43.
93. Ibid, p. 1239.
94. On the list of his publication, ibid., 1239–42.
95. Ibid., p. 1239.

2 GENERAL REMARKS ON DARWINISM

1. For Darwin's influence on the Western world: Cynthia E. Russett, *Darwin in America: The Intellectual Response 1865–1912* (San Francisco 1926); Richard Hofstadter, *Social Darwinism in American Thought* (Boston 1955); J. Dewey, *The Influence of Darwin on Philosophy* (New York 1910); S. Barnett, ed., *A Century of Darwinism* (London, 1958).
2. On those, see for example, I. Abu Lughod, *Arab Rediscovery of Europe* (Princeton 1963); Albert Hourani, *Arabic Thought in the Liberal Age, 1798–1939* (London 1962); A. L. Tibawi, *British Interests in Palestine 1800–1901* (London 1961); A. L. Tibawi, *American Interest in Palestine 1800–1901* (London, 1966); George Antonius, *The Arab Awakening*; Philip Hitti, *Lebanon in History* (New York 1952); Zeine Zeine, *The Emergence of Arab Nationalism* (Beirut 1966); H. Sharabi, *Arab Intellectuals and the West: The Formative Years, 1875–1914* (Baltimore 1970).
3. For their social and political impacts: On Muslims, see Nikki R. Keddie, *Sayyid Jamal al-Din al-Afghani* (Berkeley 1977); N. Keddie *An Islamic Response to Imperialism* (Berkeley 1968); On Christian socialism, see: Donald M. Reid, 'Syrian Christians: The Rags to Riches Story, and Free Enterprise', *International Journal of Middle East Studies*, I (October 1970), pp. 358–62; Malcom Kerr 'Notes on the Background of Arab Socialist Thought', *Journal of Contemporary History*, 3 (1968), pp. 158–65.
4. H. Spencer, *First Principles* (New York, 1891), p. 396.
5. Y. Sarruf, 'Al-Mazhab al-Darwini' (Darwin's Doctrine)' *al-Muqtataf*, 7 (1882), p. 33.

6. See a letter to the editor by Ali Yusuf, which appeared in *al-Muqtataf*, 33 (1908), pp. 878–79.
7. See two unsigned letters which appeared in *al-Hilal*, 18 (1910), p. 433 and in *al-Muqtataf*, 37 (1912), p. 95. A detailed account of the ancient Arab contribution to the idea of evolution appeared in most Arab writings on Darwinism and will be discussed in this study.
8. See his reply to Ali Yusuf in *al-Muqtataf*, 33 (1908), p. 879.
9. Rashid Rida (1865–1935) was born in Syria and later in his life moved to Egypt where he met Muhammed Abduh. He was influenced by Abduh's philosophy and became one of his disciples. In 1898, Rida launched the journal *al-Manar* which remained until his death. He wrote Abduh's biography and many other works on different aspects of Islamic religion. He defended Shumayyil's views on religion. See Daghir, *Masadir al-Dirasat*, vol. 2, p. 395.
10. Farah Antun, was born in Tripoli, Lebanon. He left for Egypt in 1897 where he founded *al-Jamiah*, a periodical that was devoted to disseminating modern French thought. In 1906, he left for New York where he resumed the publication of *al-Jamiah* for a while, before he came back to Egypt and stayed until his death in 1922. While in New York, he refuted many aspects of Afghani's *Refutation of Materialism*, a point will be considered later in this study. For more information on his life and work see, Hourani, *Arabic Thought*, pp. 253–59; Sharabi, *Arab Intellectuals*, pp. 70–79 and D. M. Reid, 'The Syrian Christians and early socialism in the Arab world', *International Journal of Middle Eastern Studies*, 5 (April, 1974), pp. 177–93.
11. R. al-Barbari, Asl al-Insan (The Origin of Man), *al-Muqtataf*, 1 (1876), pp. 242–45, 279–81.
12. Ibid., pp. 245 and 281.
13. Edwin R. Lewis (d. 1907) joined the teaching staff of the SPC in 1871 and was forced to resign as a result of his commencement speech in 1882. His speech was reported in *al-Muqtataf*, 7 (1882), pp. 158–67. The translation of Lewis's article by N. Bawarshi can be found in N. Farag's thesis, Appendix IV, pp. 406–15.
14. This crisis is usually referred to as the Lewis Affair and was competently discussed elsewhere. Thus, there is no need to repeat it here except for the relevance to our study. See the following writers:
   A. Tibawi, 'The Genesis and Early History of the Syrian Protestant College', *Middle East Journal*, 21 (1967), pp. 1–15 and 199–212; Jurji Zaydan, *al-Hilal*, 3 (1924), pp. 271–75; 4 (1925), pp. 373–76; 5 (1925), pp. 516–20; 6 (1925), pp. 637–40.
   Shafiq Jiha, 'Azmat Sanat 1882' (The Crisis of 1882), *Kitab al-Aid*, ed., J. S. Jabbur (Beirut 1967), pp. 320–39.
   Donald M. Leavitt, 'Darwinism in the Arab World: The Lewis Affair at the Syrian Protestant College', *Muslim World*, 7 (1981), pp. 85–98.
   Nadia Farag, 'The Lewis Affair and the Fortune of al-Muqtataf', *Middle Eastern Studies*, 8 (1972), pp. 73–83.
   S.B.L. Penrose, *That They May Have Life*, pp. 43–48.
   Albert Hourani, *Arabic Thought*, pp. 249–50.
15. Y. Sarruf, 'Darwinism', 7 (1882), pp. 65–73; pp. 121–27; J. Dennis,

'al-Darwiniya' (Darwinism), *al-Muqtataf*, 7 (1882–1883), pp. 233–36. A rejoinder to Dennis' article appeared in *al-Muqtataf*, 7 (1882–83), pp. 287–90; Y. al-Haik, 'Darwinism', ibid., pp. 290–92.

16. While historians nowhere mentioned Shumayyil's knowledge of the German language, Sharabi indicated that he read a French translation of Büchner's work on Darwinism. This suggests that Shumayyil's translation of Büchner into Arabic was from the French version. H. Sharabi, *Arab intellectuals*, p. 69. n. 7.

17. The complete translation of the *Origin* into Arabic was completed in 1964 after the death of Mazhar. This translation will be discussed later in this study.

18. While no writer has yet mentioned this translation, Mazhar indicated its existence in *al-Usur*, 1930, p. 36. It is conceivable that he never completed his translation and his work never appeared in Arabic.

19. This translation is the subject of discussion later in this study.

20. See n. 14 of this chapter.

3 SECULARIST CHRISTIAN RESPONSES TO DARWINISM: IDEAS AND IDEOLOGIES

1. Hourani, *Arabic thought*, p. 248.
2. Quoted by Y. Sarruf, 'Al-Doctor Shibli Shumayyil' (Dr Shibli Shumayyil), *al-Muqtataf*, 50 (1917), p. 108.
3. Sharabi, *Arab Intellectuals*, p. 69.
4. L. Mazhar, 'Shumayyil wa-Fakrat al-Tatawwur fi al-Sharq al-Arabi' (Shumayyil and the Idea of Evolution in the Arab East), *al-Kitab*, 21 (1946), p. 129.
5. S. Shumayyil, *Falsafat al-Nushu*, pp. A and 357.
6. Ibid., pp. 33–36.
7. Najm A. Bezirgan, 'The Islamic World', in Thomas F. Glick, ed., *The Comparative Reception of Darwinism* (London 1972), p. 378.
8. S. Shumayyil 'Fi al-Kahrabaiah' (On Electricity), *al-Jinan*, 1 (1871), pp. 94–96; pp. 161–64; pp. 200 –1.
9. Shumayyil, *Falsafat al-Nushu*, pp. 38–43.
10. Ibid., p. 36; see also Sharabi, *Arab Intellectuals*, p. 71.
11. Shumayyil, *Majmuat al-Doctor Shumayyil*, pp. 108–9.
12. Ibid., pp. 225 and 172.
13. The journal is named after its publishers. It was bi-monthly and published in Cairo by a Lebanese Christian, Salem Sarkis, from 1905 to 1924. See Tarazi, *Tarikh al-Sahafa*, p. 294.
14. M. Ziada, 'Doctor Shumayyil al-Shaar' (Dr Shumayyil, The Poet), *Majallat Sarkis*, 7 (1913), pp. 410–16.
15. Ibid. p. 411.
16. Ibid., p. 415.
17. Shumayyil's reply appeared in *Majallat Sarkis*, 7 (1913), p. 552.
18. Arab writers also noted Quranic studies and other theoretical subjects as science.

19. Yusuf Shalhat, 'Tanazaa al-Baqa bin al-Ulum' (A Struggle for Survival among Sciences), *al-Muqtataf*, 34 (1909), pp. 284–88.
20. Ibid., p. 288.
21. Iskandar Damanhuri 'Ayy Ashadd Tathir fi Tarqiyyat Shoun al-Ummah al-Ulum al-Tabiaya am al-Ulum al-Adabyia' (Which Has More Impact on the Progress of Nation – The Natural Sciences or Literary Sciences?), *al-Hilal*, 8 (1899), pp. 143–46.
22. Ibid., p. 144.
23. Ibid., p. 145.
24. Ibid.
25. Y. Sarruf 'Al-Doctor Shibli Shumayyil, Tarjamatu' (Dr Shibli Shumayyil, His Bibliography), *al-Muqtataf* 50 (1917), p. 109.
26. Quoted in *Majallat Sarkis*, 8 (1914), p. 617.
27. R. Rida, 'Response to Kabani's Letter to the Editor', *al-Manar*, 12 (1920), p. 635. See Shumayyil's defence of Rida on religious matters in *Falsafat al-Nushu*, p. 353, n. 1.
28. See *Majallat Sarkis*, 9 (1916), p. 174.
29. Ibid., p. 130.
30. S. Shumayyil, 'al-Falsafa, al-Maddiah wa Madhab al-Nushu' (Materialistic Philosophy and the Doctrine of Evolution), *al-Muqtataf*, 35 (1909), p. 647.
31. Ibid., p. 647, ft. 3.
32. S. Shumayyil, *Falsafat al-Nushu*, pp. 26–27.
33. Ibid., p. 28.
34. The translation can be found in S. Shumayyil, *Falsafat al-Nushu*, pp. 63–224.
35. This book is also in S. Shumayyil's *Falsafat al-Nushu*, pp. 226–307.
36. S. Shumayyil, *Falsafat al-Nushu*, pp. 28–29.
37. Ibid., p. 29.
38. S. Shumayyil, *Falsafat al-Nushu*, p. 31.
39. Ibid., pp. 39–54.
40. S. Musa, *Haula Allamuni* (Cairo 1953)..
41. Marx was not mentioned among those who influenced him.
42. See Fuad Sarruf 'Tatawwar al-Fikr al-Ilmi fi Miat Sanah (The Development of Scientific Thought in 100 Years), *in Nashat al-Arab al-Ilmi fi Miat Sanah* (Beirut, 1962) (Arab Scientific Activity in 100 Years), p. 407.
43. 'Mumayzat al-Thaqafa al-Haditha' (Features of Modern Culture), in *al-Majalla al-Jadida*, 2 (1930) p. 858.
44. Ibid., p. 860.
45. S. Musa, *Mukhtarat Salama Musa* (Cairo 1926), p. 196.
46. S. Musa, *al-Yawm wa al-Ghad*) (Cairo 1927) (Today and Tomorrow), p. 40.
47. S. Musa, *Fi al-Hayah wa al-Adab* (Cairo 1930) (Life and Literature), pp. 70–72.
48. Ibid., pp. 72–73.
49. S. Musa, editorial, *al-Majalla al-Jadida*, 1 (1929), pp. 27–28.
50. See some of Musa's publications at the end of his book, *al-Insan Qimmat al-Tatawwur* (Cairo 1961).

140   *Notes and References*

51. For example in *al-Muqtataf*, 35 (1909), pp. 727–38 and 36 (1910), pp. 437–39. In *al-Hilal*, 30 (1921), pp. 149–54.
52. S. Musa, *Haula Allamuni*, p. 39.
53. In *al-Muqtataf*, 34 (1909), pp. 570–74.
54. Ibid., p. 571.
55. Ibid.
56. Ibid., p. 573.
57. In *al-Majalla 'al-Jadida*, 2 (1930).
58. Ibid.
59. Ibid.
    By 1950, Musa admitted that he was mistaken in his convictions: 'I was under the influence of Nietzsche, who called for the obliteration of the weak. Darwin's theory on the struggle for survival and survival of the fittest became my religious belief, and it supported Nietzsche's doctrine.' See S. Musa, 'Araft al-Muqtataf Munzu Khamsin Sana' (Knowing al-Muqtataf for 50 years), *al-Muqtataf*, 117 (1950), p. 211.
60. *al-Muqtataf*, 36 (1910), pp. 437–39.
61. Ibid., p. 439.
62. Sarruf's answer, Ibid., p. 439.
63. Bezirgan, who paraphrased Shumayyil's statement, misidentified the page of his citation from Shumayyil's *Falsafat al-Nushu*. Compare Hassani, who did not detect this infelicity. See Bezirgan, 'The Islamic World', in Glick, ed., *The Comparative Reception of Darwinism*, p. 378. Hassani, *Introduction of Scientific Naturalism in England and the Arab World 1860–1930*, (Ph.D. thesis, University of Leicester, 1979), p. 284.
64. Shumayyil, *Falsafat al-Nushu*, p. 356–57.
65. *Al-Majalla al-Jadida*, 2 (1930), pp. 1240–93.
66. Ibid., p. 1293.
67. S. Musa, *Nazariyat al-Tatawwur*, p. 13.
    Musa was very happy to see the second edition of his book (which appeared in 1953) sold out in fewer than five years, while it took the first edition twenty-five years to be sold. This was clear evidence, he noted, that scientific and materialistic thought soared above metaphysical and legendary views. Ibid., p. 12.
68. Ibid., p. 18.
69. Ibid., p. 21.
70. Ibid., p. 37.
71. Ibid., pp. 90–98.
72. Ibid., pp. 166–93, pp. 193–98.
73. Ibid., pp. 184.
74. Ibid., pp. 198–242.
75. Ibid., pp. 243–54.
76. Ibid., p. 260.
77. S. Musa, *Nazariyat al-Tatawwur*, pp. 234–36.
78. S. Musa, *Mukhtarat Salama Musa*, pp. 98–103.
79. S. Musa, *Muqadimat al-Superman*, p. 2.
80. S. Musa, *Al-Yuwm wa al-Ghad*, p. 116.
81. Ibid., p. 117.
82. S. Musa, 'Al-Din wa al-Ilm' (Religion and Science), *al-Hilal*, 35 (1927), p. 813.

83. Ibid., p. 815.
84. Ibid.
85. Musa debated with other Arab scholars on many literary and linguistic subjects; see Anwar al-Gindi, *al-Musajalat wa al-Maarik al-Adabiya* (Cairo n.d.) (The Intellectual Battles in Literature).
86. S. Musa, *Haula Allamuni*, p. 161.
87. On more such terms, see *al-Muqtataf*, 66 (1922), pp. 1, 52, 103.
88. Quoted in M. Girdaq, 'Al-Doctor Sarruf Alimann' (Dr Sarruf is Scientist), *al-Muqtataf*, 72 (1928), p. 420; Y. Sarruf, 'Al-Ulum al-Tabiayyah' (The Natural Sciences), *al-Muqtataf*, 1 (1876), pp. 169–71.
89. Ibid., p. 420.
90. Tarazi, *Tarikh al-Sahafa al-Arabiyah*, p. 429.
91. Shumayyil, *Falsafat al-Nushu*, p. 23.
92. Ibid.

4 SECULARIST CHRISTIAN RESPONSES TO CONTROVERSIES ABOUT DARWINISM

1. *Al-Muqtataf*, 7 (1883), pp. 262–68.
2. Ibid., p. 262.
3. Ibid., p. 263.
4. Ibid., pp. 266–67.
5. Ibid., p. 268.
6. *Al-Muqtataf*, 48 (1916), pp. 313–19.
7. Ibid., p. 314.
8. Ibid., p. 315.
9. Amin Abu Khatir, 'Al-Intikhab al-Tabiai wa Falsafat al-Alman fi al-Harb' (Natural Selection and the German Philosophy in the War), *al-Muqtataf*, 48 (1916), pp. 327–31.
10. Ibid., p. 328.
11. Ibid.
12. Ibid., p. 330
13. Y. Sarruf, 'Al-Rojhan' (Tha name of Shumayyil's poem), *al-Muqtataf*, 48 (1916), pp. 299–300.
14. Ibid., p. 300
15. Ibid.
16. Ibid.
17. S. Shumayyil, 'Al-Falsafa al-Maddiyya: Haqiqatuha wa Nataijuha' (Materialist Philosophy: Its Truth and Its Results), *al-Muqtataf*, 48 (1916), pp. 393–97.
18. Ibid., p. 393.
19. Ibid.
20. Ibid., p. 394.
21. Ibid.
22. Ibid., p. 395.
23. Ibid.
24. Sarruf's answer to Shumayyil's letter was printed in page *al-Muqtataf*, 48 (1916), pp. 397–99.

25. Ibid., p. 397.
26. Ibid., p. 399.
27. *Al-Hilal*, 23 (1925), pp. 464–68.
28. Ibid., p. 465.
29. Ibid., p. 466.
30. Ibid., p. 467.
31. Ibid., p. 468.
32. S. Musa, 'Nazaa Jadida fi al-Ilm: Min al-Madiya ila al-Rohiyyah' (New Movement in Sciences: From Materialism to Spiritualism), *al-Hilal*, 28 (1919), pp. 132–35.
33. Ibid., p. 133.
34. Ibid.
35. Ibid., p. 134.
36. Ibid., pp. 134–35.
37. S. Musa, 'Al-Tabiaa wa al-Insaniya' (Nature and Humanity), *al-Majalla al-Jadida*, 2 (1930), pp. 1175–76.
38. Ibid., p. 1176.
39. Ibid.
40. S. Musa, 'Al-Taqim wa al-Ujinyya' (Eugenics and Sterilization), *al-Majalla al-Jadida*, 2 (1930), pp. 1474–76.
41. Hafiz Mahmud, 'Social Selection' *al-Majalla al-Jadida*, 1 (1929), pp. 109–11.
42. Ibid.
43. I. Mazhar, 'Al-Tanahur Ala al-Baqa' (The Struggle for Survival), *al-Usur*, 2 (1928), pp. 678–80.
44. Ibid., p. 679.
45. Ibid., p. 679. For more on Kropotkin's ideas, see James Allen Rogers, 'Russian Social Sciences', in Thomas Glick, ed., *The Comparative Reception of Darwinism*, pp. 256–67.
46. Ibid., p. 680. Most probably, this figure was I. Hasanyn, Deputy Minister of Education of Egypt in 1923 and his remarks on Darwin's ideas will be discussed later in this chapter.
47. Mazhar, 'From the Survival of the Fittest to the Survival of the Unfit', *al-Usur*, 6 (1930), pp. 225–32.
48. Ibid., p. 231.
49. Thomas Glick, 'Spain', in his edition, *The Comparative Reception of Darwinism*, pp. 327–29. It is interesting to mention that Chil's story could provide an analogy to Shumayyil's work in the Arab East. It seems safe to indicate that in both cases an unorthodox publication was the main reason for the diffusion of Darwinism. Moreover, while each area of the refutation was based on religious grounds, in the Arab world there was no official or religious prohibition against reading Shumayyil's work, as happened in Spain.
50. Mazhar, 'Evolution and its Impact on the Future Human Thought', *Al-Majma al-Misri lal-Thaqafa al-Ilmiya*, 1 (1930), pp. 21–55.
51. Ibid., p. 37.
52. Ibid., p. 38.
53. Ismail Hasanyn, 'Al-Taawun wa al-Talim', *al-Muqtataf*, 62 (1923), pp. 354–57; pp. 422–25 and pp. 548–53.

54. Ibid., p. 422–25 and p. 548.
55. I. Mazhar, 'Darwin wa Tanaza al-Baqa' (Darwin and the Struggle for Survival), *al-Muqtataf*, 63 (1923), pp. 60–62.
56. Ibid., p. 61.
57. Ibid., p. 62.

5 TRADITIONALIST RESPONSES TO DARWINISM

1. Ibrahim al-Yaziji (1847–1906) son of Nasif al-Yaziji, a classical Arab writer. Ibrahim's writing was mainly on Arab history and language. He launched *al-Diya* in 1898, a periodical that battled certain aspects of Darwinism with Cheikho. He supervised the Arabic translation of the Old Testament for the Jesuits. Daghir, *Masadir al-Dirasast*, vol. 11, p. 759.
2. See, for example, L. Cheikho's reply to *al-Hilal* and *al-Muqtataf* in *al-Mashriq*, 3 (1900), pp. 413–15, pp. 109–12.
3. *Al-Diya*, 1 (1899), pp. 675–79.
4. L. Cheikho, 'Al-Quwa al-Aqila fi al-Hayawan' *al-Mashriq*, 2 (1899), p. 753.
5. *New World Translation of the Holy Scriptures* (New York, 1981), p. 661 (hereafter cited as *Holy Scriptures*). This edition will be used here.
6. Ibid., p. 753.
7. Ibid., p. 754.
8. Ibid., p. 755.
9. *Al-Diya*, 2 (1899–1900), pp. 16–18.
10. Ibid., p. 17.
11. Ibid., p. 18.
12. Cheikho, 'Aql al-Hayawan' (Animal Reason), *al-Mashriq*, 2 (1899), p. 900.
13. Ibid., p. 902.
14. *Al-Mashriq*, 2 (1899), p. 996–97.
15. Saad, 'Al-Quwa al-Aqila fi al-Hayawan' (On Animal Rational Power), *al-Diya*, 2 (1899–1900), pp. 24–80, pp. 109–12.
16. Ibid., p. 80.
17. Ibid., pp. 111–12.
18. For more debate on this issue, see, for example, Father Qustantin, *al-Diya*, 2 (1899–1900), pp. 145–48, 175–79, 204–7, 239–41 and R. Saad, ibid., 1 (1898), pp. 613–16, 646–49, 677–29.
19. Cheikho, 'Nahnu wa al-Muqtataf' (We and al-Muqtataf), *al-Mashriq*, 17 (1914), pp. 695–700. cf. *al-Muqtataf*, 38 (1914), pp. 162–67.
20. Ibid., p. 696.
21. Ibid.
22. *Al-Muqtataf*, 22 (1898), p. 117.
23. *Al-Mashriq*, 1 (1898), p. 860–61.
24. Ibid., p. 861.
25. *Al-Mashriq*, 1 (1898), pp. 44–55.

26. Ibid., p. 53.
27. *The Holy Scriptures*, Joshua, 110:11, p. 265.
28. Ibid., p. 53.
29. Cheikho, 'Manna Bani Israil' (The Manna of the Israelites), *al-Mashriq*, 1 (1898), pp. 1078–83. cf. *al-Muqtataf*, 21 (1897), p. 23 and 16, (1891), p. 641.
30. Ibid., p. 1079.
31. Ibid., p. 1080.
32. Ibid., p. 1081.
33. Ibid., p. 1082.
34. Ibid., p. 1983.
35. *Al-Mashriq*, 1 (1898), pp. 1009–15. Cf. 'Tawallud al-Uqul wa-Irtiqauha' (The Genesis of Mind and its Evolution), *al-Muqtataf*, 22 (1898), pp. 246–51.
36. Ibid., p. 1010.
37. Ibid.
38. Ibid., p. 1012.
39. Faraj and Hourani's ideas on Darwinism were discussed by Najm Bezirgan, 'The Islamic World', in Thomas Glick, ed., *The Comparative Reception of Darwinism*, pp. 380–81.
40. Ibid., pp. 1–12.
41. Ibid., pp. 1–14.
42. Ibid.
43. *Al-Hilal*, 7 (1898), pp. 341–44.
44. *Al-Mashriq*, 3 (1900), pp. 1130–32, a reply to *al-Hilal*, 9 (1900), pp. 49–50.
45. Ibid., p. 1131.
46. Ibid., p. 1132.
47. *Al-Mashriq*, 2 (1899), pp. 529–32.
48. Ibid., p. 531.
49. *Al-Mashriq*, 3 (1901), pp. 1105–15.
50. Ibid., p. 1105.
51. Ibid., p. 1110–11.
52. Ibid., p. 1111.
53. *Al-Mashriq*, 3 (1900), pp. 139–40 of 'Azam al-Alat al-Falakiyah' (On Astronomical Instruments), *al-Muqtataf*, 24 (1900), pp. 1–4.
54. *Al-Mashriq*, 12 (1909), pp. 425–36.
55. On this journal, see Tarazi, *Tarikh al-Sahafa al-Arabiyah*, p. 444.
56. Ibid., p. 431.
57. Ibid.
58. Ibid.
59. What is interesting about Kais is that he had studied astronomy in Argentina and possibly even at La Plata, a highly respectable German-manned observatory at the turn of the century. Cheikho, 'al Fatawi', p. 432.
60. *Al-Mashriq*, 3 (1900), pp. 189–90. A reply to *al-Hilal*, 8 (1900).
61. Ibid., p. 190.
62. Ibid.
63. Cheikho, 'Tanqud al-Din wa al-Ilm' (Contradiction Between Science and Religion), *al-Mashriq*, 3 (1900), p. 303.

64. Ibid., pp. 303–5.
65. *The Holy Scriptures*, pp. 730 and 747. Cheikho, 'Tanqud...', p. 304.
66. *Al-Muqtataf*, 43 (1913), pp. 162–69.
67. Ibid., p. 163.
68. Ibid., pp. 164–65.
69. *Al-Mashriq*, 9 (1913), pp. 687–706.
70. Ibid., p. 689.
71. Ibid., p. 691.
72. Ibid., p. 694.
73. Ibid., p. 695.
74. *Al-Mashriq*, 21 (1923), pp. 81–92.
75. Ibid., p. 87.
76. Ibid., p. 92.
77. *Al-Mashriq*, 19 (1921), pp. 606–18, 659–70, 739–50, 814–28, 908–18.
78. Ibid., p. 609.
79. Ibid., p. 611.
80. Ibid., p. 742.
81. Ibid., p. 743.
82. *Al-Hadiyah*, 6 (1888), pp. 227–78, 7 (1889), pp. 259–62, 270, 279–80, 285–86, 293–94, 299–301.
83. Ibid., p. 227.
84. It was published by Hawawini, from 1905 to 1909. Tarazi, *Tarikh al-Sahafa al-Arabiya*, p. 426.
85. Quoted in I. Hazim, 'Shawaghl al-Fikr al-Arabi al-Masihi Mondu 1866' (Preoccupation of Arab Christian Thought since 1866), in *al-Fikr al-Arabi fi Miat Sana* (Beirut, 1967) (Arabic Thought in a Hundred Years), pp. 359–60.
86. Quoted in ibid., p. 360.
87. Y. Sarruf, 'Iftiat al-Mashriq Ala al-Muqtataf,' *al-Muqtataf*, 45 (1914), p. 167.

6 THE MUSLIM RESPONSE TO DARWINISM

1. On this point see, Hourani, *Arabic Thought*, pp. 37–38, and Ayman al-Yassini *The Relationship Between Religion and State in the Kingdom of Saudi Arabia* (Ph.D thesis, McGill University, 1982), especially chapter one.
2. Jean Lecerf, 'Le mouvement philosophique contemporain en Syrie et Egypte', *Melanges Institut française de Damas*, 1 (1929), pp. 29–64.
3. On this translation see Keddie's book: *An Islamic Response to Imperialism*, pp. 130–74.
4. Ahmad Urabi (1841–1911), born in Egypt. He was an officer in the Egyptian Army when he took power in defiance of European control of Egypt. This revolt resulted in the British occupation of Egypt in 1882. See, Daghir, *Masadir al-Dirasat*, vol. 2, p. 126,; Zaydan, *Tarajim Mashahir*, vol. 2, 55.
5. Hourani, *Arabic Thought*, p. 114.
6. Keddie, *An Islamic Response*, p. 15.

7. Ibid., p. 136.
8. Ibid., p. 135.
9. Ibid.
10. A flea in the Arabic version.
11. Ibid., p. 136.
12. Ibid. There is no evidence to suggest that Afghani ever read anything of Carl Näggeli on the inheritance of acquired characteristics, but his views on circumcision practised by Jews and Muslims were very similar to those of Näggeli. Quoted in W. M. Montgomery, 'Germany', in Glick, ed. *Comparative Reception of Darwinism*, p. 102.
13. Ibid., p. 173.
14. See Chapter 3, pp. 72–75.
15. Muhammad al-Makhzumi, *Khatirat Jamal al-Din al-Afghani* (Damascus 1965) (The Thought of al-Afghani), p. 116.
16. Born in Tripoli, Lebanon, like other Syrian intellectuals he left for Egypt in 1897 where he launched *al-Jamiah*, a secularist periodical which aimed to diffuse French thought on rationalism and revolution. He translated into Arabic Rousseau's *Emile*, Jules Simon's *La Femme du 19e siecle*, and Renan's *Vie de Jésus*. He also wrote many novels such as the famous one on *Urashalim al-Jadidah* (New Jerusalem) and *al-ilm, al-Din Wa-al-Mal* (Knowledge, Religion and Wealth). In 1906, he moved with his journal to New York; later, he moved back to Egypt and continued his intellectual work until his death in 1922. For more information on his life and work see, Donald M. Reid, *The Odyssey of Farah Antun: A Syrian Christian's Quest For Secularism* (Minneapolis 1975); A. Hourani, *Arabic Thought*, pp. 253–59; Sharabi, *Arab Intellectual*, pp. 70–79. In Arabic, see Anwar al-Jundi, *Al-Muhafazah wa al-Taqlid Fi al-Nathr al-Arabi al-Muasir* (Cairo 1961), pp. 264–69.
    Al-Jamiah (New York edition), 1 (1906), pp. 145–57, 196–202, 238–40.
18. Ibid., p. 146. Cf. Sarruf's reply on Afghani's ideas, *al-Muqtataf*, 30 (1905), p. 565.
19. Ibid., p. 151.
20. Ibid., p. 152, pp. 154–57 and p. 200.
21. Ibid., p. 239.
22. For Renan's talk see, Henriette Psichari, ed., *Ouevres complètes de E. Renan* (Paris 1947), vol. 1, pp. 945–65.
23. Afghani's answer was in French and translated by Kiddie, *An Islamic Response*, pp. 181–87.
24. Ibid., p. 183.
25. Ibid.
26. Ibid., p. 186.
27. Ibid., p. 187.
28. Muhammad al-Mukhzumi, *Khatirat al-Afghani*, pp. 114–19.
29. Ibid., p. 115.
30. Ibid.
31. Ibid., p. 118.
32. Hussein al-Jisr, *Al-Risalah*, pp. 134–56.
33. Ibid., p. 145.
34. Ibid.

35. Ibid., p. 146.
36. Ibid.
37. Ibid., pp. 156–57.
38. Ibid., p. 157.
39. Ibid., p. 162; see also pp. 162–74.
40. Ibid., p. 174.
41. Ibid., p. 178.
42. Ibid., p. 217.
43. Ibid., pp. 272–75.
44. Ibid., p. 286.
45. M. A. H. Eliasi, *The Holy Quraan* (The Burney Academy n.d.), pp. 321, 352, 522, 338.
46. Al-Jisr, *al-Risalah*, p. 298.
47. Ibid., p. 299.
48. Hourani, *Arabic Thought*, p. 223.
49. R. al-Isfahani, *Naqd Falsafat Darwin* (Baghdad 1914) (hereafter cited as *Naqd Darwin*).
50. Ibid., p. 5.
51. Ibid., p. 3.
52. Ibid., pp. 7–8.
53. Ibid., p. 6.
54. Ibid., p. 14.
55. Ibid., p. 16.
56. Ibid., p. 17.
57. Ibid., p. 21.
58. Ibid., pp. 25–27.
59. Ibid., p. 42.
60. Ibid., p. 43.
61. Ibid., p. 44.
62. Ibid., pp. 45–46.
63. Ibid., p. 53.
64. Ibid., p. 59.
65. Ibid., p. 85. Here, it seemed that Isfahani was very selective in his citations and thus refrained from mentioning those who opposed Owen's views on the mental gap between man and the ape. In fact, soon after Owen presented his findings to the British Association for the Advancement of Science in 1860, Huxley, at the same session, flatly denied Owen's ideas on man's brain, which contains a posterior lobe lacking in the apes. See F. Burkhardt, 'England and Scotland: Learned Societies', in Glick, ed., *Comparative Reception of Darwinism*, pp. 36–37.
66. Ibid.
67. Ibid., p. 86.
68. Ibid., p. 87.
69. Ibid., p. 119.
70. Ibid., p. 111.
71. Yuhana Wortabat (1827–1908) was born in Beirut of Armenian origin. He studied medicine in England. He returned to Beirut where he was appointed to teach medicine at the SPC from 1866 to 1890, see Zaydan, *Tarajim Mashahir*, vol. 2, pp. 232–37.

72. Ibid., p. 66.
73. Ibid., p. 63.
74. Ibid., p. 92.
75. Ibid., p. 72.
76. Ibid., p. 78.
77. Ibid., p. 124.
78. Ibid., pp. 124–25.
79. Ibid., p. 127.
80. Ibid., p. 130.
81. Ibid., p. 134.
82. Ibid., p. 152.
83. Ibid., p. 163.
84. Ibid., p. 173.
85. Ibid., p. 185.
86. Ibid., pp. 186–200.
87. Ibid., p. 221.
88. Ibid., p. 225.
89. Ibid., pp. 235–36.
90. Isfahani, *Naqd Falsafat Darwin* - Part Two (Baghdad 1914).
91. Ibid., p. 37.
92. Ibid., p. 55.
93. Ibid., p. 59.
94. Ibid., p. 93.
95. Ibid., pp. 117–18.
96. Ibid., p. 121. Cf. Shumayyil, *Falsafat al-Nushu*, p. 57.
97. Ibid., pp. 122–23.
98. Ibid., pp. 142–43.
99. Ibid., pp. 141–42.
100. Ibid., p. 162.
101. Mustafa al-Mansuri, *Tarikh al-Madhahib al-Ishtirakiyah* (The History of Socialist Doctrines) (Cairo 1914).
102. Ibid., p. 82.
103. Ibid., p. 83.
104. Ibid.
105. Ibid., pp. 83–84.
106. Ibid., pp. 84–85.
107. Ibid., p. 86.
108. Ibid., p. 87.
109. Ibid., p. 88.
110. Ibid., p. 90.
111. Ibid., p. 91.
112. Hassan Hussein, *Fasil al-Magal Fi Falsafat al-Nushu wa-al-Irtiqa* (On the Philosophy of Evolution and Progress) (Cairo 1924) (hereafter cited as *Introduction*).
113. See his letter to the editor where he defended miracles and revelation, *al-Muqtataf*, 65 (1924), pp. 211–12.
114. Ibid., pp. 7–8.
115. Ibid., p. 7.
116. Ibid., p. 9.

117. Ibid., p. 10.
118. Ismail Mazhar 'Fasl al-Maqal Madhahb al-Nushu fi Almania' (On Evolution's Doctrine in Germany), *al-Muqtataf*, 67 (1925), p. 75.
119. Ibid., p. 76.
120. Hussein, *Introduction*, pp. 14–15.
121. Ibid., p. 15.
122. Ibid., pp. 27–28.
123. Ibid., p. 29.
124. On this point see, Peter J. Vorzimmer, *Charles Darwin: The Years of Controversy* (Philadelphia 1970), especially pp. 71–95 on the causes of variability.
125. Hussein, *Introduction*, p. 34.
126. Mazhar, 'Fasl-Magal', p. 78.
127. M. A. H. Eliasi, *the Holy Quraan* (The Burney Academy, n.d.), XXII:47, p. 334.
128. Ibid., LXX:4, p. 564.
129. Hussein, *Introduction*, p. 26. It is interesting to note that Sayyid Muhammad, editor of the periodical *Al-Majalla al-Madrasiya* (Scholastic Journal), was a Muslim who followed Hussein's approach. He published an article entitled 'Al-Din wa al-Ulum al-Haditha' (Religion and Modern Science) which appeared in his periodical in 1903. Muhammad was surprised to find some Arab circles still of the opinion that most modern scientific subjects contradict religion and advance atheism among the population. These circles, he added, 'Make us think that these sciences were brought to our countries by foreigners for the aim of distorting religion and confusing us. On the contrary, careful understanding of modern science brings us closer to God.' *Al-Majalla al-Madrasiya*, 1 (1903), pp. 161–63. To support his point, Muhammad provided verses from the Quran which encourage people to study science. In fact, he did not discourage the study of modern science. The author quoted verses that discuss natural sciences, astronomy, chemistry, medicine, physiology, natural history, plant science, geography, geology, statistics, history, mathematics, philosophy, political science, biology, law and even linguistics.
130. Eliasi, *The Holy Quraan*, XXII:5, p. 328.
131. Ibid., XXXV:11, p. 429.
132. Hussein, *Introduction*, pp. 28–29.
133. Ibid., p. 34.
134. Ibid., p. 53.
135. Ibid., p. 61.
136. Ismail Mazhar, *Malqa al-Sabil fi Madhhab al-Nushu wa al-Irtiqa* (Cairo 1926) (hereafter cited as *Malqa al-Sabil*).
137. On his other publication and work see, Daghir, *Masadir al-Dirasat*, pp. 1237–43.
138. Mazhar, *Malqa al-Sabil*, p. 5.
139. Ismail Mazhar, 'Uslub al-Fikr al-Ilmi' (The Method of Scientific Thought), *al-Muqtataf*, 68 (1926), p. 149.
140. Ibid., p. 141.
141. Ibid.

142. Ibid., p. 142.
143. Ibid., p. 143.
144. Ibid., p. 144 and Daghir, *Masadir al-Dirasat*, p. 1239.
145. Amin al-Khuli, 'Uslub al-Fikr al-Ilmi: Naqad wa Atab' (Method of Scientific Thought: Critique), *al-Muqtataf*, 68 (1926), p. 75. Mustafa al-Shihabi, 'Hawl Usul al-Fikr al-Ilmi' (On the Method of Scientific Thought). Ibid., 68 (1926), pp. 87–88. On Mazhar's rejoinder see ibid., 69 (1927), p. 328 and 69 (1926), pp. 221–22.
146. Mazhar, 'Hurriyat al-Fikr' (Freedom of Thought), *al-Usur*, 2 (1928), p. 1179.
147. Daghir, *Masadir al-Dirasat*, p. 1238.
148. Ismail Mazhar, 'Falsafat al-Inqilab al-Turki al-Hadith' (The Philosophy of Modern Turkish Revolution), *al-Majalla al-Jadida*, 1 (1930), pp. 1212–28.
149. Ibid., pp. 1212–13.
150. Mazhar, *Malqa al-Sabil*, p. 3.
151. Ibid., p. 4.
152. M. Shihabi, 'Malqa al-Sabil fi Madhhab al-Nushu wa al-Irtiqa', *Majallat al-Majma al-Ilmi al-Arabi* (Journal of the Arab Scientific Society), 7 (1928), p. 137.
153. Mazhar, *Malqa al-Sabil*, p. 60.
154. Ibid., pp. 56–57.
155. Ibid., p. 57.
156. Ibid.
157. Ibid., p. 67.
158. Ibid., p. 62.
159. Ibid.
160. Ibid., p. 43.
161. Ibid., p. 25.
162. Ibid., p. 164.
163. Ibid., p. 197, p. 129 and p. 117.
164. Ibid., p. 165.
165. Ibid., p. 296.
166. Ismail Mazhar, *Asl al-Anwa*, an Arabic translation of the *Origin of Species* (Baghdad 1973).
167. Ibid., p. 5.
168. Ibid., p. 6.
169. Ibid., pp. 11–14.
170. Ibid., pp. 52–53.
171. David Hull, 'Darwinism and Historiography', in Glick, ed., *The Comparative Reception of Darwinism*, p. 392.
172. N. Bezirgan, 'The Islamic World', in Glick, ed., *The Comparative Reception of Darwinism*, p. 381.

CONCLUSION

1. A. Zahlan, *Science and Science Policy in the Arab World* (London 1980), p. 182.
2. A. Ziadat, 'Arab Scientists in the North American Scientific Community', *Arab Studies Quarterly*, 4 (1982), p. 245.
3. Majallat al-Doha, (November, 1982), pp. 104–9.
4. Ibid., p. 106.

Note on Source Material

This study is based on periodicals and books written in Arabic during the late nineteenth and early twentieth centuries. The books are found for the most part in the Weidener and H. Gibb libraries of Harvard University and in the Institute of Islamic Studies of McGill University.

Those who wrote on Darwinism were, then, identified with the help of the following sources:

1. Y. A. Daghir *Dictionnaire de la presse libanaise (1858–1924)* (Beirut 1978) (In Arabic).
2. Y. A. Daghir *Les Sources arabes de l'histoire de Liban* (Beirut 1972) (In Arabic).
3. Y. A. Daghir *Massadir al-Dirasah al-Adabiyah* (Beirut 1956), 3 vols (Sources of Arab studies).
4. M. Hartmann *The Arabic Press of Egypt* (London 1899).
5. J. Zaydan *Tarikh Adab al-Lughah al Arabiyah* (Cairo 1914), 4 vols (History of Arabic Language Literature).
6. *Faharis al-Mashriq al-Ammah* (Beirut 1952) (Bibliographical Dictionary).
7. Louis Cheikho *Al-Adab al-Arabiyah fi al-Quarn al-Tasi Ashar* (Beirut 1908), 2 vols (Arab Literature in the Nineteenth Century).
8. Yusuf Sarkis *Mujam al-Matbuat al-Arabiyya wa al-Muarraba* (Cairo 1928–31) (Bibliographical Dictionary on Arab Publications and Translations).
9. Faud Sarruf, ed. *Fihris al-Muqtataf* (Beirut 1967–68), 3 vols (Bibliographical Dictionary).
10. J. Zaydan *Tarajim Mashahir al-Sharq fi al-Qarn al-Tasi Ashar* (Cairo 1911).
11. Khayr al-Din Zirkili *al-Alam* (Cairo 1954–59) (Bibliographical Dictionary).
12. Abdelghani Ahmed Bioud *3200 Revues et journaux arabes de 1800 à 1965*, *titres arabes et titres translittérés* (Paris 1969).
13. Philip Tarazi *Tarikh al-Sahafa al-Arabiya* (Beirut 1914) 4 vols (History of Arabic Press).

Hartmann, Tarazi, Ahmed-Bioud and Daghir's *Presse libanaise* were excellent sources for selecting Arab scientific journals of our study period. These dictionaries not only provide the dates and the editors of journals, but also indicate whether the subject matter is scientific, literary, industrial, economic or political.

In selecting Arab science writers, I have been guided by Zaydan, Cheikho, Zirkili, Sarkis, and Daghir's *Masadir al-Dirasat*. Of particular importance are the works of Fuad Sarruf, who detailed Arab writings on Darwinism as they appeared in *al-Muqtataf*, and Daghir, who provided a section devoted to Arab scientific writings on medicine, mathematics, agriculture, and natural knowledge. *Al-Mashriq's* bibliographical dictionary included a section on intellectual conflicts among Arab thinkers which was also helpful.

It was relatively easy to assemble the published work of Arab Christian writers. For the Muslim writers who were less known to the students of the Arab nineteenth century, such as Isfahani and Hussein, the material is not as easily available. Only sketches of their writings appeared in some conservative Arab journals like *al-Mashriq*. Since the work of these Muslims writers are not available in North American libraries, a special effort was made to locate imprints in the Middle East.

Selective Bibliography

SECONDARY SOURCES

English and French Sources

Abu-Lughod, Ibrahim, *Arab Rediscovery of Europe* (Princeton 1963).
Adams, Charles, *Islam and Modernism in Egypt* (London 1933).
Antonius, George, *The Arab Awakening* (London 1939).
Banton, Michael, ed., *Darwinism and the Study of Society* (London 1961).
Baumer, F. L., *Main Currents of Western Thought* (New York 1956).
Berkes, Nigazi, *The Development of Secularism in Turkey* (Montreal 1964).
Bliss, F. J., The *Reminiscenses of Daniel Bliss* (New York 1920).
Blunt, W. S., *The Secret History of British Occupation of Egypt* (London, 1923).
Brinton, Crane, *The Shaping of Modern Thought* (Englewood Cliffs 1963).
Cromer, G., *Modern Egypt* (New York 1916), 2 vols.
Darwin, Francis, *The Life and Work of Charles Darwin* (New York 1887).
Dewey, John, *The Influence of Darwin on Philosophy* (New York 1910).
Dodge, Bayard, *Al-Azhar – A Millennium of Muslim Learning* (Washington 1961).
Dodge, Bayard, *The American University of Beirut* (Beirut 1958).
Dodwell, Henry, *The Founder of Modern Egypt, A Study of Muhammad Ali* (Cambridge 1931).
Draper, J. W., *History of the Conflict Between Religion and Science* (London 1875).
Fahmy, Moustafa, *La révolution de l'industrie en Egypt, 1800–1850* (Leiden 1954).
Frye, Richard N., ed., Islam and the West (The Hague 1957).
Gibb, H. A. R. and Bowen, Harold, *Islamic Society and the West* (London 1950), 2 vols.
Gibb, H. A. R. and Bowen, Harold, *Studies on the Civilization of Islam* (Boston 1962).
Glick, Thomas F., ed., *The Comparative Reception of Darwinism* (Austin 1972).
Gran, Peter, *Islamic Roots of Capitalism Egypt 1760–1840* (Austin 1979).
Haddad, Robert M., *Syrian Christians in Muslim Society: An Interpretation* (Princeton 1970).
Hartman, Martin, *The Arabic Press of Egypt* (London 1899).
Heyworth-Dunne, J., *An Introduction to the History of Education in Egypt* (London 1968).

154

Hitti, Philip, *Lebanon in History* (New York 1957).
Hofstadter Richard, *Social Darwinism in American Thought* (New York 1959).
Hourani, Albert, *Minorities in the Arab World* (London 1947).
Hourani, Albert, *Syria and Lebanon* (London 1954).
Hourani, Albert, *Arabic Thought in the Liberal Age* (London 1962).
Hourani, Albert, *Europe and the Middle East* (Berkeley 1980).
Issawi, Charles ed., *The Economic History of the Middle East 1800–1914* (London 1966).
Jessup, H. H., *Fifty-Three Years in Syria* (New York 1910), 2 vols.
Keddie, Nikki, *An Islamic Response to Imperialism* (Berkeley 1968).
Keddie, Nikki, *Sayyid Jamal ad-Din al-Afghani: A Political Biography* (Berkeley 1972).
Kerr, Malcom H., *Islamic Reform* (Berkeley 1966).
Kotb, Y. S., *Science and Science Education in Egyptian Society* (New York 1951).
Kuhn, T., *The Structure of the Scientific Revolutions* (Princeton 1970).
Landes, David, *Bankers and Pashas* (London 1958).
Lerner, Daniel *The Passing of Traditional Society* (New York 1958).
Lewis, Bernard, *The Emergence of Modern Turkey* (London 1968).
Lewis, Bernard, *The Middle East and the West* (New York 1964).
McFarland, T., *Daily Journalism in the Arab States* (Columbus 1953).
Mathews, R. D. and Akrawi, M., *Education in Arab Country of the Near East* (Washington 1949).
Munro, John, *A Mutual Concern – The Story of the American University of Beirut* (New York 1977).
Penrose, Stephen, *That They May Have Life* (New York 1941).
Polk, William, ed., *Beginnings of Modernization in the Middle East* (Chicago 1968).
Qubain, Fahim, *Education and Science in the Arab World* (Baltimore 1966).
Russet, Cynthia, *Darwin in America* (San Francisco 1976).
Salibi, K. S., *The Modern History of Lebanon* (New York 1965).
Schuman, L. O., *The Education of Salama Musa* (Leiden 1961).
Sharabi, Hisham, *Arab Intellectuals and the West 1875–1914* (Baltimore 1970).
Smith, Wilfred C., *Islam in Modern History* (New York 1963).
Tamim, Suha, *A Bibliography of AUB Faculty Publications, 1866–1966* (Beirut 1967).
Tibawi, A. L., *American Interests in Syria 1800–1901* (London 1966).
Tibawi, A. L., *British Interests in Palestine 1800–1901* (London 1961).
Tibawi, A. L., *Islamic Education* (London 1972).
Tignor, E. L., *Modernization and British Colonial Rule in Egypt* (Princeton 1966).
Vanderpool, H. Y., *Darwin and Darwinism* (London 1973).
Vatikiotis, P. T., *The Modern History of Egypt* (New York 1969).
Zeine, N. Zeine, *Arab Turkish Relations and Emergence of Arab Nationalism* (Beirut 1966).

Representative Arabic Books

Abd al-Karim, Ahmad, *Tarikh al-Talim Fi Asr Muhammad Ali* (History of Education in the Age of Muhammad Ali) (Cairo 1938).
Al-Bustani, B., *Muhit al-Muhit* (Beirut 1870).
Amin, Ahmad, *Zuama al-Islah Fi al-Asr al-Hadith* (Leaders of Reform in the Modern Era) (Cairo 1948).
Al-Dibs, Y. M., *Tarikh Suriya* (History of Syria) (Beirut 1907).
Husayn, Taha, *Mustagbal al-Thaqafah Fi Misr* (The Future of Culture in Egypt) (Cairo 1938).
Khuri, R., *Al-Fikr al-Arabi al-Hadith* (Modern Arab Thought) (Beirut 1943).
Al-Makhzumi, M., *Khatirat Jamal al-Din al-Afghani* (Thought of Jamal al-Din al-Afghani) (Cairo 1931).
Ridwan, A. F., *Tarikh Matbaat Bulaq* (History of the Bulaq Press) (Cairo 1953).
Al-Rifaai, S., *Tarikh al-Sahafa al-Suriya* (History of the Syrian Press) (Cairo 1917).
Sami, A., *Al-Talim Fi Misr* (Education in Egypt) (Cairo 1917).
Cheikho, L., *Al-Adab al-Arabiyah fi al-Qarn al-Tasi Asher* (Arabic Literature in the Nineteenth Century) (Beirut 1924).
Al-Yasoay, B., *Al-Faraid* (Arab-French Dictionary) (Beirut n.d.).
Rida, Rashid, *Tarikh al-Ustad al-Imam al-Shaykh Muhammad Abduh* (Cairo 1931).
Sharabi, H., *Al-Muthagafon al-Arab Wa al-Gharb* (Arab Intellectuals and the West) (Jerusalem 1978).
Sabat, Halil, *Tarikh al-Tibaa fi al-Sharq al-Arabi* (Cairo 1966).
Al-Yaziji, K., *Rowwad al-Nahda al-Adabiya* (Pioneers of Arab Literature) (Beirut 1962).

Essays and Papers

Arabic

Faris, Nabih, 'Al-Madrasa al-Kulliya' (The School-College), *al-Abhath*, 20 (1967), pp. 323–55.
Farris, Nabin, 'Saff 1883 fi al-Madrassa al-Kulliya', *al-Abhath*, 21 (1968), pp. 39–55.
Jiha, S. 'Azamat Sant 1882' (The Crisis of 1882), *Kitab al-Id*, ed. Jabbur, J. S. (Beirut 1967).
Khouri, Yusuf, 'Cornelius van Dyck: Mualafatuh al-Ilmiya (Cornelius van Dyck: His Scientific Publications), *al-Abhath*, 18 (1965), pp. 389–418.
Seraj al-din, Ahmed, 'Al-Haraka al-Tarbawya fi Lubnan wa Suria' (Educational Movement in Lebanon and Syria), *al-Abhath*, 19 (1966), pp. 330–40.

English and French

Alain, Silvera, 'The First Egyptian Mission to France under Muhammad Ali', *Middle Eastern Studies*, 16 (1980), pp. 1–22.

Faraj, Nadia, 'The Lewis Affair and the Fortune of al-Muqtataf', *Middle Eastern Studies*, 8 (1972), pp. 72–83.

Heyworth-Dunne, J., 'Printing and Translation under Muhammad Ali of Egypt: The Foundation of Modern Arabic', *Journal of the Royal Asiatic Society*, 3 (London 1940), pp. 325–49.

Hitti, Philip, 'The Impact of the West on Syria and Lebanon in the Nineteenth Century', *Cahiers d'histoire mondiale*, 2 (1955) pp. 609–15.

Lewis, B., 'The Impact of the French Revolution on Turkey', *Cahiers d'histoire mondiale*, 1 (1953), pp. 105–25.

Musa, Matti, 'Yaqub Sanu and the Rise of Arab Drama in Egypt', *International Journal of Middle Eastern Studies*, 5 (1974), pp. 401–33.

Reid, D., 'Syrian Christians, the Rages to Riches Story and Free Enterprise', *International Journal of Middle Eastern Studies*, 1 (1970), pp. 358–67.

Reid, D., 'The Syrian Christians and Early Socialism in the Arab World', *International Journal of Middle Eastern Studies* 5 (1974), pp. 177–93.

Saadi, Lutfi, 'Al-Hakim Cornelius van Allen van Dyck (1818–1895)', *Isis*, 27 (1937), pp. 20–45.

Saadi, Lufti, 'The Life and Work of George Edward Post (1838–1909)', *Isis*, 28 (1938), pp. 385–417.

Tibawi, A. L., 'The Genesis and Early History of the Syrian Protestant College', *Middle East Journal*, 21 (1967), pp. 1–12.

Ziadat, Adel, 'Arab Scientists in the North American Scientific Community', *Arab Studies Quarterly*, 4 (1982), pp. 242–53.

PRIMARY SOURCES

Arabic Books

Al-Afghani, Jamal al-Din, *Al-Radd ala Dahriyyin* (Refutation of Materialists) (Cairo 1955).

Cheikho, Louis, *Al-Adab al-Arabiyah Fi al-Qarn al-Tasi Ashar,* 2 vols (Arab Literature in the Nineteenth Century) (Beirut 1908).

Daghir, Y. I., *Masadir al-Dirasah al-Adabiyah*, 3 vols (Sources of Arab Studies) (Beirut 1956).

Daghir, Y. I., *Kamous al Sahafah al-Lubnaniyah (1858–1924)* (Dictionary of Lebanese Press) (Beirut 1978).

Hussein, Hassan, *Fasil al-Maqal Fi Falsafat al-Nushu Wa al-Irtiqa* (On the Theory of Evolution and Progress) (Cairo 1924), a translation of Ernest Haeckel's *Commentary on the Theory of Evolution.*

Al-Isfahani, M. R., *Naqd Falsafat Darwin*, 2 vols (Critics of Darwin's Philosophy) (Baghdad 1914).

Al-Jisr, Hussein, *al-Risala al-Hamidiyya fi Haqiqat al-Diana al-Islamiyyah wa Haqiqat al-Sharia al-Muhamadiyya* (A Hamedian Essay on the Truthfulness of Islamic Religion and the Truthfulness of Islamic Canon Laws) (Beirut 1887).

Al-Mansuri, H., *Tarikh al-Madhahb al-Istirakiyah* (History of Socialist Doctrines) (Cairo 1915).

Mazhar, Ismail, *Asl al-Anwa* (The Origin of the Species (Baghdad 1973), an Arabic translation of Darwin's *Origin of Species*.

Mazhar, Ismail, *Malqa al-Sabil Fi Madhhab al-Nushu wa al-Irtiqa* (The Doctrine of Evolution and Progress) (Cairo 1924).

Musa, Salama, *al-Insan Quimmat al-Tatwwur* (Man is the Acme of Evolution) (Cairo 1961).

Musa, Salama, *Muqdimat al-Superman* (The Advent of Superman) (Cairo 1909).

Musa, Salama, *Nazariyyat al-Tatawwur wa asl al-Insan* (The Theory of Evolution and the Origin of Man) (Cairo 1928).

Musa, Salama, *Haula Allamuni* (Those Who Taught Me) (Cairo 1930).

Musa, Salama, *al-Yawm wa al-Ghad* (Today and Tomorrow) (Cairo 1928).

Musa, Salama, *Tarbiyat Salama Musa* (The Education of Salama Musa) (Cairo, 1947).

Musa, Salama, *Fi al-Hayah wa al-Adab* (Cairo, 1930).

Sarkis, Yusuf, *Mujam al-Matbuat al-Arabiyya wa al-Muarraba* Bibliographical Dictionary on Arab Publications and Translations) (Cairo 1928–31).

Sarruf, Faud, ed., *Fihris al-Muqtataf*, 3 vols (Bibliographical Dictionary) (Beirut 1967–68).

Shumayyil, Shibli, *Majmuat al-Doctor Shibli Shumayyil*, 2 vols (Cairo 1910).

Shumayyil, Shibli, *Falsafat al-Nushu wa al-Irtiqa* (Theory of Evolution and Progress) (Cairo 1910).

Tarazi, Philip, *Tarikh al-Sahafa al-Arabiyah*, 4 vols (History of the Arabic) Press), (Beirut 1914).

Zaydan, Jurji, *Tarikh Adab al-Lughah al-Arabiyah*, 4 vols. (History of Arabic Literature) (Cairo 1914).

Zaydan, Jurji, *Tarajim Mashahir al-Sharq fi al-Qarn al-Tasi Ashar*, 2 vols (Biographies of Prominent Arabs) (Cairo 1902).

Zaydan, Jurji, *al-Lugha al-Arabiyyah Kain Hayy* (Cairo, 1904).

Zirkili, K. A., *al-Alam* (Bibliographical Dictionary) Cairo 1954–59).

Arabic Newspapers and Periodicals

Name of Periodical   *Years Consulted*

Amal al-Majma al-Ilmi al-Arabi	1920–30
al-Bashir	1880
al-Bayan	1898
al-Diya	1898–1906
al-Hadiya	1887–88
al-Hilal	1892–1930
al-Irfan	1909–30
al-Jamiah	1899–1908
al-Jinan	1870–85
al-Manar	1898–1930
Majallat Sarkis	1905–20
al-Majalla al-Jadida	1927–30
al-Majalla al-Shahriyya	1903
Majallat al-Majma al-Ilmi al-Sharqi	1883–84
al-Majma al-Misri Lal-Thaqafa al-Ilmiya	1929–30
al-Majalla al-Madrasiya	1903
al-Mashriq	1898–1930
al-Muqtataf	1876–1930
al-Shifa	1886–92
al-Thaqafah	1927–30
al-Usur	1927–30
Yacoup al-Tib	1865–67
al-Abhath	1965–67
al-Doha	1982

UNPUBLISHED MATERIALS

Faraj, Nadia, *Al-Muqtataf 1876–1900: A Study of the Influence of Victorian Thought on Modern Arabic Thought* (Oxford University, Ph.D thesis, 1969).

Hassani, A., *The Comparative Reception of Scientific Naturalism in England and the Arab World 1860–1930* (University of Leicester, Ph.D. thesis, 1979).

Al-Yassini, Ayman, *The Relationship Between Religion and State in the Kingdom of Saudi Arabia* (McGill University, Ph. D. thesis, 1982).

Index